MW01281901

THE
VITAL
GROUPS

Witness Lee

Living Stream Ministry
Anaheim, CA • www.lsm.org

First Edition, December 1996.

ISBN 978-1-57593-815-8

Published by

Living Stream Ministry
2431 W. La Palma Ave., Anaheim, CA 92801 U.S.A.
P. O. Box 2121, Anaheim, CA 92814 U.S.A.

Printed in the United States of America

10 11 12 13 14 / 10 9 8 7 6 5

CONTENTS

PREFACE

This book is composed of messages given by Brother Witness Lee in Anaheim, California from August 21 through December 11, 1996.

THE VITAL GROUPS

MESSAGE ONE

THE PURPOSE OF THE VITAL GROUPS

Scripture Reading: Matt. 18:15-22; 2 Tim. 2:22; Rom. 14:17; Eph. 2:14-17; 2 Pet. 1:8

OUTLINE

I. To live the kingdom life—Matt. 18:15-22:
   A. The kingdom life is the God-man life.
   B. What is covered in Matthew 18:15-22 unveils to us how to take care of a sinning brother in a vital group:
      1. Go and reprove him between you and him alone. If he hears you, you have gained your brother—v. 15.
      2. If he does not hear you, take with you one or two more, that by the mouth of two or three witnesses every word may be established—v. 16.
      3. If he refuses to hear them, tell it to the church—v. 17a.
      4. If he refuses to hear the church also, the vital group should pray by exercising the authority of the church, which is the authority of the kingdom—vv. 17b-18; 16:18-19.
      5. Dealing with such a situation by the vital group in harmony with the Lord in their midst—vv. 19-20.
      6. With a forgiving spirit—vv. 21-22.
      7. By this way the vital groups live the God-man life as Christ did when He was living on the earth.

II. To live the church life—2 Tim. 2:22:
  A. Pursuing righteousness, faith, love, peace with those who call on the Lord out of a pure heart.
  B. The kingdom life is practiced and realized in the church life—Rom. 14:17.
  C. We must live the kingdom life according to Matthew 5 through 7; then we can live the church life:
    1. By pursuing:
      a. Righteousness—to take care of God's righteous way—Rom. 14:17a.
      b. Faith—to take care of God's faithfulness.
      c. Love—to take care of God's heart.
      d. Peace—to take care of God's peace in producing the church for our relationship with others in the church—Eph. 2:14-17; Rom. 14:17b.
    2. Through the calling on the Lord out of a pure heart—seeking nothing but the Lord only, without ambition or any other greediness.
    3. Such a pursuing, existing in the vital group and abounding, constitutes the vital group neither idle nor unfruitful (John 15:5, 16) unto the full knowledge of our Lord Jesus Christ—2 Pet. 1:8.
    4. Thus, the vital groups can live the normal church life, overcoming the degradation of the church, to constitute the Body of Christ for the consummation of the New Jerusalem, the goal of God's eternal economy:
      a. By exercising our regenerated spirit of power, love, and sobermindedness—2 Tim. 1:7.
      b. By holding in faith and love the healthy words received from the apostle and guarding the good deposit through the indwelling Spirit—1:13-14.
      c. By cutting straight the word of the truth—2:15.
      d. By enjoying the Lord in our spirit as the abiding grace—4:22.

I am thankful to the Lord that He has restored this fellowship on the vital groups. This has been frustrated by Satan for more than two years. In this message we want to see the purpose of the vital groups in their intrinsic significance. The purpose of the vital groups is to live two kinds of lives: the kingdom life and the church life. We must repent and admit that we have defects in these two kinds of lives. Even though we may have been in the recovery for years, we have not seen that the vital groups are for living the kingdom life and the church life.

The New Testament revelation is concerning these two lives. The center of the four Gospels is the kingdom. Matthew and John are the two books that take the lead to touch the truth of the kingdom. Matthew's main point is the kingdom of the heavens, and the main point touched by John is the kingdom of God. John, of course, is a Gospel of life, but life brings us into the kingdom of God. We are regenerated into the kingdom of God. If we are not born anew, we cannot see or enter into the kingdom of God (John 3:3, 5). In the Epistles, including Acts, the center is the church life.

When we practiced the church life in mainland China before 1949, we had only home meetings, not group meetings. This practice started in Shanghai and brought in much blessing. Then when the Lord brought us to Taiwan, we realized that just to have the home meetings was insufficient, so we began to have group meetings. The Lord's blessing on us was rich and abounding. Some in Korea in 1958 followed us to have this practice, but instead of using the word *groups,* they used the word *cells.* The body is built up by the cells. Our practice of the group meetings in Taiwan was a great factor of increase. Within four years, we increased from about three to five hundred as a beginning to fifty thousand. In the United States we adopted the practice of the groups, but the groups have entered into a dormant situation. After studying our situation, we realize that our groups are not vital.

The scriptural base for our teaching concerning the practice of the vital group meetings is in Matthew 18:15-22 and 2 Timothy 2:22. Matthew 18:15-22 teaches us how to have small groups in the kingdom life. Then 2 Timothy 2:22 teaches us how to have a church life in the degradation of the church.

I. TO LIVE THE KINGDOM LIFE

We need to read and consider prayerfully the Lord's speaking in Matthew 18:15-22, which reveals how we can live the kingdom life. Verses 15 through 17 say, "Moreover if your brother sins against you, go, reprove him between you and him alone. If he hears you, you have gained your brother. But if he does not hear you, take with you one or two more, that by the mouth of two or three witnesses every word may be established. And if he refuses to hear them, tell it to the church; and if he refuses to hear the church also, let him be to you just like the Gentile and the tax collector." If this sinning one would not listen even to the church, what shall we do? The text says that we should let him be to us like the Gentile and the tax collector, that is, like an unsaved person who is outside the fellowship of the church.

Verse 18 then says, "Truly I say to you, Whatever you bind on the earth shall have been bound in heaven, and whatever you loose on the earth shall have been loosed in heaven." We have to see the connection between verses 17 and 18. Verse 17 is so low, saying that we should let the sinning one who will not listen to the church be to us like a Gentile and a tax collector. But verse 18 says that we should touch heaven by our binding and releasing prayer. This is the prayer of the vital group. Verse 19 says, "Again, truly I say to you that if two of you are in harmony on earth concerning any matter for which they ask, it will be done for them from My Father who is in the heavens." This is the practice of a vital group of two or three in harmony touching the very God in heaven. These are the two or three mentioned in verse 16: "But if he does not hear you, take with you one or two more...." These are the members of a vital group.

If a brother sins against us, we need to deal with him first in love. If we cannot get through, we should bring with us one or two more to contact him. If we still cannot get through, we should tell it to the church, and if the church cannot get through, then the sinner brother will lose the fellowship of the church. But this is not all. We have to then pray in the way of binding and releasing, and we have to pray in harmony. Whatever we pray, our Father in heaven will accomplish to gain that person. Verse 20 says, "For where there are two or three gathered into My name, there am I in their midst." This is the reality of the vital groups. These two or three are gathered into the Lord's name for His purpose, not into their names for their purposes.

Many times we feel that a certain saint is a hopeless case, and we stop with this feeling toward him in our small groups. We always end our small group meeting in verse 17. We would not take Christ as the heavenly ladder in verse 18 to climb up to the heavens with prayer that binds Satan and looses the sinning brother. We and the church may have no way with this brother, but should we give him up? The Lord Jesus said that we should let him be to us like a Gentile and a tax collector. But the Lord went on to say that we have to bind Satan. We have to bind the binding one and release the bound one by praying together in harmony.

We should not bring in any opinions by uncovering the fallen condition of the one for whom we are praying. We have to bind the binding one, Satan, and we have to release the sinning one, the one bound by Satan, through our prayer in harmony. To be in harmony is as musical sounds in harmony. When a piano is played properly, the many keys on the piano are struck in such a way so as to produce harmonious music. When we pray in harmony for certain backsliding, sinning ones, our prayer to recover them becomes like music to the ears of the Father in heaven.

After the Lord spoke this word, Peter came to the Lord to ask Him a question. Verses 21 through 22 say, "Then Peter came and said to Him, Lord, how often shall my brother sin against me and I forgive him? Up to seven times? Jesus said to him, I do not say to you, Up to seven times, but, Up to seventy times seven." It may have been that Peter was the one against whom a brother sinned. He did not want to forgive this brother again, so he asked the Lord, "How many times should I forgive him? Seven times?" The Lord said that

Peter should forgive him seventy times seven, or four hundred ninety times. If we have a spirit to forgive a sinning one up to four hundred ninety times, surely that one will be recovered. Do we who are participating in the vital groups have such a spirit?

Our vital group may be reducing instead of increasing. Where are the others? Perhaps some have become degraded or backslidden and others are offended. We may have a reason for each one no longer meeting with us, but would the Lord agree with our reasoning? The Lord would ask, "Where is your brother?" In other words, the Lord would not let us give people up. We should not give up on anyone. We have to go to the Lord again and again with prayers touching heaven by binding and releasing in harmony. *Heaven* means God. We touch God, and God comes in to do something. This is what it means to live the kingdom life.

If someone wrongs us, we should not be offended but still love him. We should not go to others to talk about his case. Instead, we should go to him alone. We should cover his situation by going to him directly. But if he would not listen to us, we have to take with us one or two more to see him. Eventually, we may have to tell the church. This is the way of the kingdom life in Matthew 18, but we do not practice this. When people sin against us, we talk to our spouse or other saints about it. This is wrong.

The first lesson we must learn as members of the vital groups is not to uncover people's weaknesses. The story of Ham in Genesis 9 is an illustration of this. His father Noah became drunk, and he was uncovered in his tent. Ham saw his father Noah's nakedness and told his two brothers about it. But his brothers, Shem and Japheth, took a garment, walked backward, and covered the nakedness of their father. As a result of this, Ham was cursed but his brothers received the blessing (vv. 20-27). In the vital groups, we have to avoid this kind of uncovering talk. Our uncovering talk is a defect that will kill our vital groups. We must learn to cover others. When we become aware of someone sinning or of someone sinning against us, we should not talk to others but to the person directly. Our natural man always likes to tell others about a person's sins or mistakes. This is wrong.

The Lord gave us the step-by-step way in Matthew 18. These steps are to go to the person alone, then with one or two others, and finally to the church. If he even would not listen to the church, would we give up? We may stop with verse 17 of Matthew 18 by simply letting him be to us like a Gentile and a tax collector. If we stop here, however, our group will be reducing instead of increasing. Following verse 17 is verse 18 where the Lord said that we have to learn to bind and to release. We have to learn to pray in harmony for a sinning one. Then the Father in heaven will perform what we ask and will be in our midst. We also have to learn to forgive others countless times. This is the reality of the vital groups.

Paul in 1 Corinthians 5 rebuked the Corinthian believers and charged them to remove a wicked one from their midst (v. 13). Paul's charge was somewhat comparable to that of the Mosaic law in the Old Testament (see Deut. 13:5; 17:7, 12; 21:21; 22:21-22, 24; 24:7). But in 2 Corinthians Paul was tender, cautious, and considerate regarding this sinful person. After Paul told the saints to remove him, he did not have the peace, so he sent Titus to see the situation. Titus brought back the good news that this wicked man repented (7:6-13). Then Paul said that the saints should forgive and comfort this one. Otherwise, they could be taken advantage of by Satan (2:6-11).

A vital group is a real representation of the church. The church should learn how to deal with a sinning one by the example of Paul. Paul did not have the peace when this sinful one was removed, so he still did something to take care of the situation. The most important thing is to cherish and forgive. To visit is to cherish. Paul sent Titus to visit Corinth in order to cherish the Corinthians. Then Paul told them to forgive. Forgiving should follow cherishing. Then we can recover and gain people.

A. The God-man Life

The kingdom life is the God-man life.

B. How to Take Care of a Sinning Brother
in a Vital Group

In summary, what is covered in Matthew 18:15-22 unveils to us how to take care of a sinning brother in a vital group. You should go and reprove him between you and him alone. If he hears you, you have gained your brother (v. 15). If he does not hear you, take with you one or two more, that by the mouth of two or three witnesses every word may be established (v. 16). If he refuses to hear them, tell it to the church (v. 17a). If he refuses to hear the church also, the vital group should pray by exercising the authority of the church, which is the authority of the kingdom (vv. 17b-18; 16:18-19). Such a situation is dealt with by the vital group in harmony with the Lord in their midst (vv. 19-20) with a forgiving spirit (vv. 21-22). By this way the vital groups live the God-man life as Christ did when He was living on the earth.

II. TO LIVE THE CHURCH LIFE

A. Pursuing Righteousness, Faith, Love, Peace
with Those Who Call on the Lord
out of a Pure Heart

The purpose of the vital groups is also to live the church life. Second Timothy 2:22 says, "But flee youthful lusts, and pursue righteousness, faith, love, peace with those who call on the Lord out of a pure heart." This is the way to live the church life by the vital groups.

B. The Kingdom Life Being Practiced
and Realized in the Church Life

Paul said in Romans 14:17 that the kingdom of God is not a matter of eating and drinking but of righteousness, peace, and joy in the Holy Spirit. This kingdom life is practiced and realized in the church life.

C. Living the Church Life
by Living the Kingdom Life

We must live the kingdom life according to Matthew 5 through 7. Then we can live the church life.

1. By Pursuing

a. Righteousness

We live the church life by pursuing righteousness. To pursue righteousness is to take care of God's righteous way. Matthew 5:20 says that unless our righteousness surpasses that of the scribes and the Pharisees, we shall by no means enter into the kingdom of the heavens. The kingdom is a matter of righteousness (Rom. 14:17a), and according to the Epistles, this surpassing righteousness is Christ Himself lived out from us (Phil. 3:9). We have to live out Christ as our righteousness.

b. Faith

To pursue faith is to take care of God's faithfulness. Hebrews 11:6 says that without faith it is impossible to be well pleasing to God. Also, when we come to God, we must believe that God is and we are not and that He is a rewarder of those who seek Him diligently. We should pursue faith that links us with God. We must be a person linked with God.

c. Love

To pursue love is to take care of God's heart. Love maintains our relationship with others. Paul taught us in 1 Corinthians 13 that among faith, hope, and love, love is the greatest (v. 13). In 8:1 Paul said that knowledge puffs up but love builds up. To forgive people is a matter of love. To visit people repeatedly without being disappointed or disheartened is also a matter of love.

d. Peace

To pursue peace is to take care of God's peace in producing the church for our relationship with others in the church (Eph. 2:14-17; Rom. 14:17b). Ephesians 2:14 through 17 says that Christ crucified all the different ordinances in order to make peace. Our opinion is a kind of ordinance. All the ordinances have been crucified, so we can have peace. The church life in the vital groups needs peace. Christians are divided because there is no peace among them due to their many opinions and concepts. Without peace we become fruitless. We are branches of Christ as the vine tree. We should bear fruit, but fruitfulness depends upon our peace. If the branches fight one another, how can they bear fruit? Our fruit-bearing is killed by different opinions.

2. Through the Calling on the Lord out of a Pure Heart

We pursue the Lord as righteousness, faith, love, and peace through calling on Him out of a pure heart, seeking nothing but the Lord only, without ambition or any other greediness. We express our opinion because we are ambitious. We want to be something in the church or be the leader in our small group. We need a pure heart to live the church life.

3. Being Neither Idle nor Unfruitful

Such a pursuing, existing in the vital group and abounding, constitutes the vital group neither idle nor unfruitful (John 15:5, 16) unto the full knowledge of our Lord Jesus Christ (2 Pet. 1:8).

4. Living the Normal Church Life

Thus, the vital groups can live the normal church life, overcoming the degradation of the church, to constitute the Body of Christ for the consummation of the New Jerusalem, the goal of God's eternal economy. If we live the kingdom life and the church life, we will overcome the degradation of the church. Today our problem is not just Satan, sin, the world, the flesh, and the self. We are facing another strong factor, that is, the degradation of the church. Actually, we were born into the degradation of the church and have been under the influence of this degradation. Second Timothy is a book dealing with the degradation of the church. It says that the saints in Asia forsook the apostle Paul (1:15). Actually, they forsook the apostolic teaching, so they began to degrade. This is why Paul wrote his second Epistle to Timothy.

a. By Exercising Our Regenerated Spirit

We can live the normal church life and overcome the church's degradation by exercising our regenerated spirit of power, love, and sobermindedness (2 Tim. 1:7). We have to fan our spirit into flame (v. 6). Our spirit of sobermindedness and power also needs to be of love. We will not let anyone go or give up on anyone when we exercise such a forgiving and loving spirit.

b. By Holding the Healthy Words and Guarding the Good Deposit

Also, we need to hold a pattern of the healthy words we received from the apostle, in faith and love, and guard the good deposit through the indwelling Spirit (2 Tim. 1:13-14). This is the deposit of the riches of the word, which we guard with the Spirit of God who indwells us.

c. By Cutting Straight the Word of the Truth

Second Timothy 2:15 says that we need to cut straight the word of the truth. This cutting is as a carpenter cuts a piece of wood. We should cut the word in a straight way. This is to unfold the word of God in its various parts rightly and straightly without distortion.

d. By Enjoying the Lord in Our Spirit as the Abiding Grace

In order to overcome the degradation of the church, we must enjoy the Lord in our spirit as the abiding grace. Christ today is the life-giving Spirit indwelling our spirit. Second Timothy 4:22, the last verse of this Epistle, says, "The Lord be with your spirit. Grace be with you." Thus, the end of this Epistle on how to deal with the degradation of the church is that we must enjoy Christ in our spirit as our abiding grace. This is the way to live the church life in the vital groups under the degradation of the church.

We must live a proper kingdom life, and the kingdom life actually is the church life. Without the kingdom life, there is no possibility to have the church life. The Lord said that whoever would follow Him must deny himself and bear the cross (Matt. 16:24). This is the reality of the kingdom life. It is a life of always denying ourselves in order to kill our natural man with all its preferences. Everything of the old man should go to the cross. Then we can have the kingdom life and the righteousness that surpasses that of the scribes and Pharisees. This righteousness is Christ living out of us as the kingdom life which becomes the church life.

THE VITAL GROUPS

MESSAGE TWO

THE CONSTITUENTS OF THE VITAL GROUPS

(1)

Scripture Reading: John 3:15-16; Matt. 5:1; 28:19; Acts 1:8

OUTLINE

I. The believers in Christ—John 3:15-16:
   A. Transferred from Adam into Christ—1 Cor. 15:22.
   B. Regenerated to be a new creation in Christ and all the old things have been washed away—2 Cor. 5:17; Titus 3:5.
   C. United with Christ in His eternal life—a union in the divine life.
   D. Joined to Christ to be one spirit with Him—1 Cor. 6:17.

II. The disciples of Christ (Matt. 5:1; 28:19), discipled through:
   A. Christ's human living on the earth, as the model of a God-man—living God by denying Himself in humanity (John 5:19, 30), revolutionizing their concept concerning man (Phil. 3:10; 1:21a).
   B. Christ's crucifixion to annul their human life for them to live the divine life—Gal. 2:20.
   C. Christ's resurrection:
      1. To know Him as God's firstborn Son—Rom. 1:4; Acts 13:33; Rom. 8:29.
      2. To know Him as the life-giving Spirit—1 Cor. 15:45.
      3. For the producing of the many sons of God as His multiplication and increase—Heb. 2:10; John 12:24.

III. The witnesses of Christ—Acts 1:8:
   A. Witnessing that:
      1. Christ had resurrected—Acts 1:22; 3:15; 10:39-41; 13:31.
      2. The resurrected Christ was anointed by God to carry out His commission—Acts 10:38-39.
      3. The resurrected Christ was made by God:
         a. The Lord and Christ (Messiah)—Acts 2:32-36.
         b. The Leader and Savior—Acts 5:30-32.
         c. The Judge of the living and the dead—Acts 10:42.
   B. Living Christ—Acts 22:15; Phil. 1:21a; 2 Cor. 13:3:
      1. In His resurrection—Phil. 3:10a.
      2. Through His death—Phil. 3:10b.

The constituents of the vital groups are six categories of persons. In this message we will cover the first three categories: the believers in Christ, the disciples of Christ, and the witnesses of Christ. In the next message we will fellowship concerning the members of Christ, the brothers of Christ, and the prophets of God.

I. THE BELIEVERS IN CHRIST

We may feel that *the believers in Christ* is a common term, but actually we do not fully realize what a believer is.

A. Transferred from Adam into Christ

The believers in Christ (John 3:15-16) have been transferred from Adam into Christ (1 Cor. 15:22). Before we were regenerated, we were in the Adamic realm. The entire world with billions of people is in Adam. Adam is a big realm, but our regeneration has transferred us out of Adam and into Christ. Christ today is our realm. Physically, we are in the United States, but actually we are in Christ.

B. Regenerated to Be a New Creation

We also have been regenerated to be a new creation in Christ and all the old things have been washed away (2 Cor. 5:17; Titus 3:5). Not only has our outward realm changed, but also our inward nature has been changed through regeneration. I was generated to be Chinese ninety-one years ago, but one day I was regenerated. We have to emphasize the syllable "*re-*". We have been regenerated to be a new creation in Christ. If we see these truths, we will realize that we are abnormal in our experience. We have been transferred out of Adam, but we still do many things in Adam and not in Christ. We were regenerated to be a new creation, but we still remain in our living as the old creation. When we became a new creation, all the old things were washed away. But this washing is also a continual process throughout our Christian life. I am concerned that many of our old concepts have not been washed away. Titus 3:5 reveals that regeneration is a great washing. We have been saved by the washing of regeneration, which is a kind of reconditioning, remaking, or remodeling with life to make us altogether new.

Our group meetings are not vital because much of the time we meet in the way of the old creation. The things of the old creation can remain with us prevailingly. Many of us come together as a "free" group instead of a vital group. We are free to talk about many things. One brother may ask another brother who cuts his hair. We should not talk about the cutting of our hair but about the cutting, the crucifying, of the flesh. We should not be so free in our group meetings. We must be restricted to the Spirit. Vital groups are composed of people in the new creation who speak about the new creation, not about the old creation.

C. United with Christ

The believers in Christ have been united with Christ in His eternal life, which is a union in the divine life. This is an organic union.

D. Joined to Christ

We are also joined to Christ to be one spirit with Him (1 Cor. 6:17). Many Christians today do not realize that Christ is the life-giving Spirit and that we are joined to Christ to be one spirit. This means that we become spirit. "That which is born of the Spirit is spirit" (John 3:6b). We have been born of the Spirit to be spirit. When we come to the vital groups, we should come in this status.

II. THE DISCIPLES OF CHRIST, DISCIPLED THROUGH CHRIST'S HUMAN LIVING, CRUCIFIXION, AND RESURRECTION

The constituents of the vital groups are the disciples of Christ (Matt. 5:1). In Matthew 28:19 the Lord Jesus said to His disciples, "Go therefore and disciple all the nations." The nations here are the Gentiles. To disciple the Gentiles is to constitute the Gentiles into the disciples of Christ. The Lord Jesus, in particular, discipled four people of two families: Peter and Andrew and James and John. He discipled them for about three and a half years. They followed the Lord and stayed with Him day and night, traveling with Him, eating with Him, and doing everything with Him. They were living with Him and were around Him all the time. They saw how this God-man behaved. They observed Him. He was a Jew, who no doubt bore a Jewish countenance. He had Jewish blood and Jewish flesh with the human life and nature. But He lived by another life in His human life. This other life is the divine life. Because He lived the divine life in His human life, His human life became mystical, a mystery. Out from His human life came something divine.

Whatever the Lord did on earth in those three and a half years was a sign, signifying something (John 2:11, note 2). Every miracle is a sign. The Lord's feeding of the five thousand with five loaves and two fish was a miracle. The disciples must have been excited when they saw such a great thing, but afterward the Lord directed them to pick up all the fragments which were left over. That was also a sign (Matt. 14:20, note 1). The Lord was divine and mystical. He did and said everything as a sign.

In John 8 a sinful woman was brought to the Lord. Eventually, He said to her, "Has no one condemned you?" (v. 10). "And she said, No one, Lord. And Jesus said, Neither do I condemn you; go, and from now on sin no more" (v. 11). This was also a sign. The Lord Jesus was God expressed, yet He would not condemn a sinner. Is this not something mystical? He was a divine and mystical person living in the divine and mystical realm, doing everything in a divine and mystical way. We should be such persons. If we are working in an office, those around us should have the feeling that there is something extraordinary about us. This extraordinary thing is divine and mystical. We all need to be discipled by the Lord to be divine and mystical persons.

By the Lord's mercy, I was able to write *Hymns,* #203 because of the Lord's discipling. Stanza 4 of this hymn says:

> We're Thy total reproduction,
>   Thy dear Body and Thy Bride,
> Thine expression and Thy fullness,
>   For Thee ever to abide.

We are Thy continuation,
Thy life-increase and Thy spread,
Thy full growth and Thy rich surplus,
One with Thee, our glorious Head.

I wrote this hymn in my sixties, after I had been discipled by the Lord for about forty years.

The disciples who followed the Lord for three and a half years saw what He did, how He behaved, and how He spoke. That discipled them. They saw Christ's human living, His death on the cross for six hours, and they saw Him in resurrection. Christ used these three processes—His human living, His all-inclusive, all-terminating, life-releasing, and new-man-creating death, and His life-dispensing resurrection—to disciple His followers.

In resurrection He became the life-giving Spirit and entered into them. He breathed Himself into them, saying, "Receive the Holy Spirit" (John 20:22). In Genesis 2 God formed man from the dust of the ground and breathed into man the breath of life (v. 7). This caused man to become living, that is, a living person. On the day of His resurrection Christ breathed Himself into His disciples and they also became living. They were made alive with the divine life. The Spirit of life and of reality who was breathed into them would guide them into all the reality of what they had observed of the Lord when they were with Him for three and a half years. I was in the recovery observing how Brother Watchman Nee acted for eighteen years. All that I observed in him became things discipling me.

A. Christ's Human Living

The followers of Christ were discipled through Christ's human living on the earth, as the model of a God-man—living God by denying Himself in humanity (John 5:19, 30), revolutionizing their concept concerning man (Phil. 3:10; 1:21a). The concept of the disciples was revolutionized by what they saw of the Lord Jesus living God by denying Himself in His humanity.

B. Christ's Crucifixion

They were discipled through Christ's crucifixion to annul their human life for them to live the divine life (Gal. 2:20).

C. Christ's Resurrection

1. To Know Him as God's Firstborn Son

They were also discipled through Christ's resurrection to know Him as God's firstborn Son (Rom. 1:4; Acts 13:33; Rom. 8:29). As the only begotten Son of God, Christ had only the divine life and nature. He had nothing human. But as the firstborn Son of God, He is both divine and human. Christ had the human life and nature, but He lived the divine life and nature through the denying of His human life and nature. This was His divine and mystical living to disciple all His followers for three and a half years.

2. To Know Him as the Life-giving Spirit

They were also discipled to know Christ as the life-giving Spirit (1 Cor. 15:45).

3. For the Producing of the Many Sons of God

Christ's resurrection was for the producing of the many sons of God as His multiplication and increase (Heb. 2:10; John 12:24).

If we open to the Spirit within us as we prayerfully consider this fellowship, we will be discipled. Only the discipled ones are the constituents of the vital groups. They have been discipled to be vital. A disciple is one who lives the divine life in his human life. The vitality of the ministry is due to a person's living the divine life out of his human life. Then what he utters is divine out of a crucified human life. We need to deny our human life for the releasing of something divine. This is the main factor of our being vital.

III. THE WITNESSES OF CHRIST

Eventually, we are the witnesses of Christ. In Acts 1:8 the Lord told the disciples, "You shall be My witnesses both in Jerusalem and in all Judea and Samaria and unto the uttermost part of the earth." A witness is one who has seen something. After Paul was saved on the road to Damascus, the Lord appointed Paul to be His witness (Acts 26:16).

A. Witnessing

1. Christ Having Resurrected

The disciples witnessed that Christ had resurrected (Acts 1:22; 3:15; 10:39-41; 13:31). If we witness that Christ has resurrected, we must live a resurrected life.

2. Anointed by God

The resurrected Christ was anointed by God to carry out His commission (Acts 10:38-39).

3. The Resurrected Christ Being Made by God the Lord and Christ, the Leader and Savior, and the Judge of the Living and the Dead

The resurrected Christ was made by God the Lord of the whole earth and the Christ, the Messiah, for carrying out God's economy (Acts 2:32-36). He was also made the Leader and Savior (Acts 5:30-32). He is the Ruler of the kings of the earth (Rev. 1:5) and the One who controls the whole earth to arrange the situation so that His chosen ones may believe into Him as their Savior to be saved. Also in His resurrection He was made by God the Judge of the living and the dead (Acts 10:42). He will judge the living on His throne of glory (Matt. 25:31-46), and He will judge the dead on the great white throne (Rev. 20:11-15).

B. Living Christ

The crucial point of the witnesses of Christ is that they live Christ (Acts 22:15; Phil. 1:21a; 2 Cor. 13:3) in His resurrection and through His death (Phil. 3:10). They do not merely preach or speak about Christ, but they live a life which witnesses Christ.

The constituents of the vital groups are the believers in Christ, the disciples of Christ, and the witnesses of Christ. All of the full-time trainees need to realize that they are being discipled by Christ's human living, by His all-inclusive death, and by His life-dispensing resurrection. After the training they should go out not just to teach, preach, and propagate but to witness. By the Lord's mercy, I have been discipled for about seventy years, and I am still under the Lord's discipling today.

THE VITAL GROUPS

MESSAGE THREE

THE CONSTITUENTS OF THE VITAL GROUPS

(2)

Scripture Reading: Rom. 12:5; 8:29; John 20:17; 1 Cor. 14:1, 31

OUTLINE

IV. The members of Christ—Rom. 12:5:
  A. The organic salvation of God is with Christ as the center and His Body as the spreading.
  B. The members of Christ constitute His Body for His spreading by His multiplication.
  C. Christ's multiplication is by Him as:
    1. A grain of wheat producing many grains—John 12:24.
    2. The vine tree bearing much fruit as His multiplication through His branches (members)—John 15:5.
  D. Such multiplications spread God through speaking for the increase of Christ (His bride)—John 3:29-30:
    1. He speaks the words of God for the dispensing of the Spirit without measure—John 3:34.
    2. His words spoken by Him and received by His believers minister spirit and life—John 6:63.

V. The brothers of Christ—Rom. 8:29; John 20:17:
  A. In His New Testament economy, the speaking God speaks in the Son—Heb. 1:2.
  B. The divine sonship of glory (Rom. 8:15, 23; John 17:22) is corporate, consisting of:
    1. Christ as the firstborn Son of God—Rom. 8:29.
    2. His believers as the many sons of God—Heb. 2:10.

C. As the firstborn Son of God being the Word of God (John 1:1) is God's oracle for the speaking and dispensing of God to carry out His eternal economy, so the many sons of God being members of the Word of God are God's oracle speaking and dispensing God for the spreading of God and the increase of Christ.

VI. The prophets of God—1 Cor. 14:1, 31:

A. Since all the sons of God are God's oracle, they become God's prophets, the ones who speak God, speak for God, and speak forth God.

B. According to 1 Corinthians 14 the meetings of the believers should be meetings for God's speaking.

C. The first verse of this chapter says that we should pursue love and desire earnestly and especially that we may prophesy, speaking God, speaking for God, and speaking forth God.

D. Verse 31 says that all the believers can prophesy, speaking God, speaking for God, and speaking forth God, one by one.

E. Verses 3 through 4 unveil to us that prophesying, speaking God, speaking for God, and speaking forth God, builds up, encourages, and consoles people.

F. Verse 5 says that the apostle Paul desired especially that we would prophesy, speaking God, speaking for God, and speaking forth God, and that greater is he who prophesies, speaking God, speaking for God, and speaking forth God.

G. For this reason God desires all men to be saved and to come to the full knowledge of the truth, that they may prophesy, speaking God, speaking for God, and speaking forth God—1 Tim. 2:4.

H. Hence, we, the believers as the sons of God to be the prophets of God, should speak God's word in season and out of season for the carrying out of God's eternal economy—2 Tim. 4:2.

In the previous message we saw the first three items of the constituents of the vital groups: the believers in Christ, the disciples of Christ, and the witnesses of Christ. In message one we pointed out that to live the church life, we have to pursue with those who call on the name of the Lord out of a pure heart (2 Tim. 2:22). Also, we have to learn how to enjoy Christ as the Spirit in our spirit to be the abiding grace for our enjoyment (4:22). We have to ask ourselves if we practice this day by day. In our daily living, do we enjoy Christ as the life-giving Spirit in our spirit to be the abiding grace for our enjoyment? We may pray for this, but do we practice our prayer? We have to admit that we have not allowed the Lord to fully disciple us in this aspect.

The apostle Peter was born a typical Jew. His concept was altogether Jewish, and he was a fisherman. But one day the divine and mystical One, Jesus, came to him. The Lord Jesus was so captivating in a mysterious way. When He told Peter to come after Him, he immediately left his work and followed Him (Matt. 4:18-20). Jesus spent time with Peter day and night for three and a half years in order to disciple him to be as He was, a God-man. Jesus was a man, even a Jew, but He lived something divine. Peter's concept was changed to fish for men, to gain men for God's economy.

We may be able to say that we need to live the divine life by denying our natural life. We may be eloquent speakers, but do we live such a life? I am thankful to the Lord that He will not let us go. He disciples the sinners and tax collectors to make them God-men who live Christ. He is discipling us so that we can be the genuine constituents of the vital groups. In this message we want to see the last three items of these constituents: the members of Christ, the brothers of Christ, and the prophets of God.

IV. THE MEMBERS OF CHRIST

After we have been discipled to be Christ's witnesses, we are qualified to be His members. Romans 12:5 says, "So we who are many are one body in Christ, and individually members one of another." As Christ's members, we are a part of Him.

A. The Organic Salvation of God Being with Christ as the Center and His Body as the Spreading

The organic salvation of God is with Christ, the Head, as the center, and His Body as the spreading.

B. Constituting His Body

The members of Christ constitute His Body for His spreading by His multiplication. We in the Lord's recovery are spreading Christ for His multiplication, but our rate of multiplication has not been that high. Christ is great, so He needs a great Body with many members through His multiplication. We should remember these two words: *spreading* and *multiplication.*

C. Christ's Multiplication

1. A Grain of Wheat

Christ's multiplication is by Him as a grain of wheat producing many grains (John 12:24). He is the unique original grain, and we are the many grains. In our function we should be the same as Christ for His multiplication.

2. The Vine Tree

In John 15 the Lord said, "I am the vine; you are the branches" (v. 5). The branches are not for blossoming but for bearing fruit. Christ as the vine tree bears much fruit as His multiplication through His branches, His members.

D. Spreading God through Speaking

The multiplication of Christ spreads God through speaking for the increase of Christ, His bride. John the Baptist said, "He who has the bride is the bridegroom....He must increase, but I must decrease" (John 3:29-30). This increase is the bride.

1. Speaking the Words of God

Christ speaks the words of God for the dispensing of the

Spirit without measure (John 3:34). Our speaking must be followed by the Spirit for dispensing.

2. *Ministering Spirit and Life*

His words spoken by Him and received by His believers minister spirit and life (John 6:63). When God's words spoken by us are received into others' spirits, they become spirit and life to them. Christ's multiplication spreads God through His speaking and our speaking. His speaking and our speaking should be the same. They should be followed by the Spirit. Christ is the Word of God, and we are the members of Christ. Therefore, we are members of the Word of God. As such we must be the oracle of God, the speaking ones, to spread God for the multiplication and increase of Christ.

V. THE BROTHERS OF CHRIST

The constituents of the vital groups are also the brothers of Christ. Romans 8:29 says that Christ is the Firstborn among many brothers. In John 20:17 the resurrected Christ told Mary, "Go to My brothers." Before His resurrection Christ never called His disciples His brothers. But in resurrection He recognized that all of His disciples were His brothers. He is the firstborn Son of God and we are the many sons of God, His many brothers.

A. Speaking in the Son

In His New Testament economy, the speaking God speaks in the Son (Heb. 1:2).

B. The Divine Sonship of Glory Being Corporate

The divine sonship of glory is a corporate matter. Romans 8:15 and 23 speak of the sonship. Then John 17:22 gives us the definition of the sonship. The sonship is the divine right to express God in His life and nature for His glory. The divine sonship of glory is corporate, consisting of Christ as the first-born Son of God (Rom. 8:29) and His believers as the many sons of God (Heb. 2:10).

C. The Many Sons of God Being Members
of the Word of God to Be God's Oracle

As the firstborn Son of God being the Word of God (John 1:1) is God's oracle for the speaking and dispensing of God to carry out His eternal economy, so the many sons of God being members of the Word of God are God's oracle speaking and dispensing God for the spreading of God and the increase of Christ. The firstborn Son of God is the oracle of God, and we are the many sons. This means that all the sons are God's oracle so that God may have a spread and Christ may have an increase.

VI. THE PROPHETS OF GOD

A. The Ones Who Speak God,
Speak for God, and Speak Forth God

The constituents of the vital groups are also the prophets of God (1 Cor. 14:1, 31). Since all the sons of God are God's oracle, they become God's prophets, the ones who speak God, speak for God, and speak forth God. A prophet is a speaking one. The Greek word for *prophesy* means to speak for or speak forth.

B. Meetings for God's Speaking

According to 1 Corinthians 14 the meetings of the believers should be meetings for God's speaking. The meetings in Christianity are for one speaker to speak, but according to 1 Corinthians 14, all the saints should be speakers (vv. 26, 31).

C. Desiring Earnestly to Prophesy

The first verse of 1 Corinthians 14 says that we should pursue love and desire earnestly spiritual gifts, but especially that we may prophesy, speaking God, speaking for God, and speaking forth God.

D. All Can Prophesy

First Corinthians 14:31 says that all the believers can prophesy, speaking God, speaking for God, and speaking forth God, one by one. I am concerned that many of us have never spoken in a church meeting. We may use only our eyes and ears in the meeting, and leave our mouth at home. We have to exercise our spirit and use our mouth in the meetings to speak for the Lord.

E. Building Up, Encouraging, and Consoling

Verses 3 through 4 unveil to us that prophesying, speaking God, speaking for God, and speaking forth God, builds up, encourages, and consoles people.

F. Paul Desiring Especially That We Would Prophesy

Verse 5 says that the apostle Paul desired especially that we would prophesy, speaking God, speaking for God, and speaking forth God, and that greater is he who prophesies, speaking God, speaking for God, and speaking forth God.

G. God Desiring All Men to Be Saved and to Come to the Full Knowledge of the Truth That They May Prophesy

For this reason God desires all men to be saved and to come to the full knowledge of the truth, that they may prophesy, speaking God, speaking for God, and speaking forth God (1 Tim. 2:4). We cannot and do not speak because we do not have the knowledge of the truth. We need to come to the full knowledge of God's Word, His truth, that we may prophesy.

H. Speaking God's Word in Season and out of Season

Hence, we, the believers as the sons of God to be the prophets of God, should speak God's word in season and out of season for the carrying out of God's eternal economy (2 Tim. 4:2).

In this message and the previous message we have seen six aspects of the constituents of the vital groups. First, we are the believers in Christ, who are transferred out of Adam into Christ, regenerated to be the new creation, united with Christ in the divine life, and joined to Christ as one spirit.

Also, we are the disciples of Christ. We all need to be discipled to be God-men.

Peter was a Jewish fisherman, not a God-man. But Christ called Peter with the intention of discipling him from being a Jew to being a God-man. The One who called Peter, Jesus Christ, was a God-man. He was a Jew, but He did not live a Jewish life. He lived the divine life by denying His Jewish life. Living the divine life made Him divine. Denying the Jewish life made Him mystical. Thus, He was a man in the divine, mystical realm. Peter was in the Jewish, natural realm, but Christ called him with the intention of discipling him for three and a half years to show him what kind of man he should be.

We should not be Jewish men, Chinese men, or American men, but God-men. To disciple a Jew into a God-man is a marvelous doing. The Lord Jesus knew that this would not be a fast work. He knew that it needed three and a half years. He charged Peter to follow Him so that Peter could observe what He did, how He lived, and how He spoke. Apparently Jesus was a Jew, but actually He lived the divine life by denying the Jewish life. This was the way He discipled His followers.

They also saw how He was crucified and resurrected. They saw a God-man living the divine life by denying the natural life through being crucified and resurrected. On the evening of the day of Christ's resurrection, the disciples were meeting in sorrow and fear. Suddenly, Jesus came and stood in their midst and said, "Peace be to you" (John 20:19). Then He breathed into them and said, "Receive the Holy Spirit" (v. 22). At that time He entered into the disciples. Before that time Peter frequently spoke in a foolish way. But after the Lord breathed Himself into Peter and poured out His Spirit upon him to empower him, Peter gave a marvelous message on the day of Pentecost.

In the four Gospels we see Jesus living the life of a God-man, and in Acts we see the disciples also living such a life. Because they had been discipled by the Lord, He told them that they would be His witnesses. They were also the members of Christ, the parts of Christ, to spread God, multiply Christ, and increase Christ. Three critical words in this message are *spreading, multiplication,* and *increase.* God's spreading, Christ's multiplication, and Christ's increase are by our speaking the word of God to dispense Christ as life for the producing and building up of the Body of Christ.

The disciples became the oracle of God, the speaking sons of God. The Lord Jesus spoke continually in His earthly ministry. Some of His marvelous speaking is recorded in Matthew 5 through 7, 13, and 24 through 25 and in John 14 through 16 plus His prayer in chapter seventeen. He was the speaking Son of the speaking God. He was God's oracle, and all His brothers, the many saints, are the same. Thus, we are the speaking sons of the speaking God. Eventually, we all become God's prophets, who speak God, speak for God, and speak forth God for the edifying of the saints and the building up of the church, the Body of Christ, to consummate the New Jerusalem for the accomplishment of God's eternal economy. We need to be discipled by the Lord with all the points of these messages.

THE VITAL GROUPS

GOD'S NEW CREATION BECOMING GOD'S ORACLE FOR HIS DISPENSING AND SPREADING

OUTLINE

I. As the constituents of the vital groups, we need to remember and realize that we are God's regenerated new creation, united with Christ in His divine life, joined to Christ as one spirit.

II. Discipled from being a natural man to being a God-man, living the divine life by denying our natural life according to the model of Christ as the first God-man.

III. Becoming the witnesses of Christ to magnify Him by living Him.

IV. To be the members of Christ constituting an organism for His increase through His multiplication.

V. To be His brothers participating with Him in the divine sonship with the divine right to express God mainly through speaking for the dispensing of God through His oracle.

VI. In God's oracle becoming the prophets of God speaking God, speaking for God, and speaking forth God.

VII. For the fruit-bearing of God's multiplication and spreading.

VIII. Through contacting people by shepherding them:

A. According to God's love toward the fallen human race.

B. Following the steps of the processed Triune God in seeking and gaining the fallen people:

1. The Son as the shepherd seeking the one lost sheep.

2. The Spirit as the woman seeking the lost coin.
3. The Father as the father of the prodigal son waiting and looking to receive the prodigal son's returning to his father's house.

In this message we want to see that God's new creation becomes His oracle for His dispensing and spreading. The word *oracle* refers to God's speaking, to the persons who carry out God's speaking, or to the place of God's speaking. The ones who were used by the Lord to write the Bible were God's oracle. Among them, Moses was great and Paul was even greater. They were persons speaking for God. Also, what they wrote and spoke was God's oracle, God's speaking. In ancient times the cover of the ark was the oracle, the place where God spoke to His people. This cover was called the mercy seat, or the propitiation cover, covering all the defects of God's people (Exo. 25:16-22). God took that place, that center, as His speaking base to speak to His people. In the New Testament the apostle Paul was one who was always in the reality of the Holy of Holies within the ark, signifying Christ. Christ with His judicial redemption has become the very place where God speaks to His people, and this place is the oracle (Rom. 3:24-25). Today in the Lord's recovery there are not only God's speaking and the speaking ones for God but also Christ with His judicial redemption as God's oracle. Since 1922 there has been God's continual speaking, His oracle, in His recovery.

I. GOD'S REGENERATED NEW CREATION

As the constituents of the vital groups, we need to remember and realize that we are God's regenerated new creation, united with Christ in His divine life, joined to Christ as one spirit (2 Cor. 5:17; 1 Cor. 6:17). We are not merely generated persons in the old creation. We have been generated twice. The first time was by our parents to be the old creation. We were generated to be the natural man, but one day we were regenerated. Our birth certificate is an important and official document which records the date of our physical birth. Our second birth certificate of our spiritual birth is seen in Romans 8:16, which says that the Spirit witnesses with our spirit that we are the children of God. Our birth certificate is a double spirit, the Spirit with our spirit.

II. DISCIPLED FROM BEING A NATURAL MAN
TO BEING A GOD-MAN

We are being discipled from being a natural man to being a God-man, living the divine life by denying our natural life according to the model of Christ as the first God-man (Matt. 28:19). The young people have come to the full-time training not to be trained in the human understanding, but to be discipled in the divine understanding. While I am helping them to be discipled, I am also being discipled day by day in many aspects to live the divine life by denying my natural life.

We should live such a life according to the model of Christ as the first God-man. When Christ was on this earth, He denied His natural life, Himself. He said that whatever He spoke was not His word but the word of the Father who sent Him (John 14:24). He never did anything out of Himself (5:19, 30). He did everything out of and by the sending Father. He was not the Sender but the Sent One. He did not live Himself; instead, He lived the Sender, the Father (6:57a). This is the model of the first God-man.

There has never been such a man in all of human history. Abraham and Moses were good, but they were not God-men. After God's incarnation there was a particular man on earth who was a God-man. This God-man did not live His human life. Instead, He lived the divine life, God Himself, by denying His human life. The Lord called some to follow Him just to see how He lived so that He could show them the pattern of a God-man. For three and a half years they saw and were discipled by this pattern. In the church life we are also being discipled by the Lord. The church life is a discipling life to disciple us from being a natural man to being a God-man. God does not care whether you are a good man or a bad man, because everything of our natural man, good or bad, must go to the cross. All the natural persons should be discipled to the cross because we have another Person in us. We have another life and nature, both divine, according to which we must live.

III. BECOMING THE WITNESSES OF CHRIST

By the Lord's discipling we become the witnesses of Christ

to magnify Him by living Him (Acts 1:8; Phil. 1:19-21a). Are we the real witnesses of Christ in our daily life? Many of the sisters are very concerned about their hairstyle and about the way their hair looks. They spend much time in front of the mirror to care for their hair. Is this the conduct of a witness of Christ? We must be His witnesses in our whole being.

Paul was such a witness. After he was saved on the way to Damascus, the Lord sent Ananias to him. Ananias said to Paul, "You will be a witness to Him unto all men of the things which you have seen and heard" (Acts 22:15). When people saw Paul, they saw Christ. He was really worthy to say, "I am crucified with Christ; and it is no longer I who live, but it is Christ who lives in me" (Gal. 2:20a). By the bountiful supply of the Spirit of Jesus Christ, Paul lived Christ in order to magnify Him. He desired to magnify Christ through life and through death (Phil. 1:19-21). Every day Paul was a demonstration, a display, of Christ to show and present the exalted Christ to others. In his living Paul was Christ because to him to live was Christ. We have to be discipled to such an extent that we become such a living witness.

IV. TO BE THE MEMBERS OF CHRIST

We are the members of Christ, constituting an organism for His increase through His multiplication (Rom. 12:5; John 15:5). Because we are Christ's members, we are a part of Him. We are members of Christ, not individualistically, but corporately. I have been in the United States for over thirty-three years, and I have always tried to practice ministering Christ, not individualistically, but with my co-workers. This is for Christ's increase. Christ must be multiplied so that He can have an increase. In John 3 the bride is the increase of the Bridegroom (vv. 29-30), just as Eve was the increase of Adam.

V. TO BE HIS BROTHERS

We are His brothers participating with Him in the divine sonship with the divine right to express God mainly through speaking for the dispensing of God through His oracle (Rom. 8:29; Heb. 1:2). The Lord Jesus was with the disciples for three and a half years, but He never called them His brothers until after His resurrection. When He resurrected, He told Mary, "Go to My brothers and say to them, I ascend to My Father and your Father, and My God and your God" (John 20:17). Through regeneration in resurrection, we all became His brothers (1 Pet. 1:3). His resurrection was a great delivery of Himself as the firstborn Son of God and of us as His many brothers, the many sons of God. We are His brothers, sharing in His divine sonship.

VI. BECOMING THE PROPHETS OF GOD

In God's oracle we become the prophets of God speaking God, speaking for God, and speaking forth God (1 Cor. 14:1, 31).

VII. FOR FRUIT-BEARING

Our speaking for God is for the fruit-bearing of God's multiplication and spreading (John 15:5). A tree multiplies and spreads by bearing fruit.

VIII. THROUGH CONTACTING PEOPLE BY SHEPHERDING THEM

We bear fruit through contacting people by shepherding them. We should be those who are always shepherding and teaching by speaking forth Christ to others. All the apostles are top speakers of the word of God. While they are speaking the word of God, they also shepherd the saints, the churches, and their co-workers. Paul especially was a pattern of one who taught and shepherded people. In 1 Timothy 3:2 Paul said that the elders should be "apt to teach." Then in 1 Timothy 5:17 he said that the elders who labor in word and teaching are worthy of double honor. All of us should follow this pattern of speaking for God and shepherding others.

A. According to God's Love

Our shepherding should be according to God's love toward the fallen human race. The fallen human race is joined with Satan to be his world in his system, but God has a heart of love toward these people.

B. Following the Steps of the Processed Triune God in Seeking and Gaining the Fallen People

My burden in this message is that we have to learn of the apostles, the elders, and even of the Triune God. We have to follow the steps of the processed Triune God in His seeking and gaining fallen people. Luke 15 records that the Pharisees and scribes criticized the Lord by saying, "This man welcomes sinners and eats with them" (v. 2). Then the Lord told three wonderful parables, which unveil the saving love of the Triune God toward sinners.

1. The Son as the Shepherd Seeking the One Lost Sheep

The Son as the shepherd would leave the ninety-nine to seek the one lost sheep (Luke 15:3-7).

2. The Spirit as the Woman Seeking the Lost Coin

The second parable is that of a woman seeking a lost coin (vv. 8-10). This signifies the Spirit seeking a lost sinner. The Son's finding took place outside the sinner and was completed at the cross through His redemptive death. The Spirit's seeking is inward and is carried out by His working within the repenting sinner.

3. The Father as the Father of the Prodigal Son

Because of the Son's step of seeking the sinner by dying on the cross and the Spirit's step of sanctifying by searching and cleansing the sinner's inward parts, the sinner comes to his senses. This is shown by the prodigal son's coming to himself and desiring to return to his father (vv. 17-18). First Peter 1:2 reveals that before we received the sprinkling of Christ's blood, the Holy Spirit sanctified us. This is His seeking sanctification. The sinner is awakened by the Spirit's seeking to cause him to return to the Father. When the prodigal son returned, his father saw him while he was still a long way off. This indicates that the father was expectantly waiting and watching day by day for his son to return. When his father saw him, he ran to receive his returning son (Luke 15:20).

This shows that God the Father runs to receive the returning sinners.

I hope that there will be a genuine revival among us by our receiving this burden of shepherding. If all the churches receive this teaching to participate in Christ's wonderful shepherding, there will be a big revival in the recovery. In the past we did much speaking and teaching with very little shepherding. Shepherding and teaching should be like two feet for our move with the Lord. Our shepherding should always be with teaching, and our teaching should always be with shepherding.

We have seen from our crystallization-study of the Gospel of John that its last chapter, John 21, reveals the apostolic ministry in cooperation with Christ's heavenly ministry. In His heavenly ministry Christ is shepherding people, and we need to cooperate with Him by shepherding people. Without shepherding, our work for the Lord cannot be effective. We must learn all the truths so that we may have something to speak and go to contact people to shepherd them.

Shepherding is something divine. In order to be a shepherd, we must be a witness of Christ, a member of Christ, and a brother of Christ, sharing His sonship. Then we will participate in the oracle of the sonship to become a prophet. As a prophet for God's oracle, we will speak for the Lord. Meanwhile, we need to shepherd people. This is the way to be fruitful, to have the multiplication and the increase. If this kind of fellowship is received by us, I believe there will be a big revival on the earth, not by a few spiritual giants but by the many members of Christ's Body being shepherds who follow the steps of the processed Triune God in seeking and gaining fallen people.

THE VITAL GROUPS

THE GREAT COMMISSION
OF CHRIST IN RESURRECTION

Scripture Reading: Acts 1:2-3; Matt. 28:16-20; Mark 16:15; Luke 24:47; Acts 2:32-36; 5:30-32; 22:15; 1:8

OUTLINE

I. The Christ in resurrection:
   A. The Christ in His incarnation:
      1. To bring God into man, making God and man as one.
      2. To live in the human life to express God, especially to express the attributes of God in His human virtues.
      3. To accomplish the all-terminating and all-redeeming death to close His ministry in His incarnation.
   B. The Christ in His resurrection:
      1. Through His death Christ entered into His resurrection to carry out His ministry in the stage of His inclusion.
      2. Through all the believers in Him as His Body to accomplish God's eternal economy.

II. The commission of Christ:
   A. After Christ entered into His resurrection from the stage of His incarnation into the stage of His inclusion, He remained among His apostles for forty days to prepare them for carrying out His heavenly ministry in His resurrection—Acts 1:2-3.
   B. At the close of His forty days' preparation of the apostles, He gave them His great commission.

C. With all authority in heaven and on earth given to Him—Matt. 28:18.

D. The eleven apostles received the great commission of Christ not only as apostles but also as disciples—Matt. 28:16:

1. To disciple the nations and teach them the teachings of Christ—Matt. 28:19-20.

2. To proclaim the gospel to all the creation—Mark 16:15.

3. To proclaim repentance for forgiveness of sins—Luke 24:47.

4. To witness a resurrected Christ appointed by God to be the Lord and Christ (Messiah), the anointed One of God, and to be the Ruler and Savior—Acts 2:32-36; 5:30-32.

5. To witness Christ, to magnify Christ, to display Christ—Acts 22:15.

6. To save and gather in all God's chosen people from Jerusalem through Judea and Samaria and unto the uttermost part of the earth—all the world, all the nations—Acts 1:8; Mark 16:15; Luke 24:47.

The content of this message is much more difficult than that of the foregoing ones. Many in the past have used the term *the great commission* to describe the Lord's charge to His disciples before He ascended. But in this message we want to pick up a deeper understanding and application of this term. The great commission of Christ is in resurrection. *In resurrection* is a critical phrase. Christ's commission is found nowhere else except in resurrection. Outside of His resurrection He has no commission. The Christ who gave the great commission is the One in resurrection. He is not only in resurrection; He Himself is resurrection. In John 11:25 the Lord Jesus said, "I am the resurrection and the life."

I. THE CHRIST IN RESURRECTION

In order to see what resurrection is, we need to see that the Lord's ministry in its history has three stages. This is new light to us from the Lord. We call these three stages the three *i*'s: incarnation, inclusion, and intensification. The first stage is the stage of incarnation, from His human birth to His death. In that stage the Lord was in the flesh, but He worked and moved by the leading of the Spirit. First, He was conceived in Mary's womb by and with the Spirit (Matt. 1:18, 20). Then Matthew 4:1 says that Christ was led by the Spirit to the wilderness to be tempted by Satan. Matthew 12:28 reveals that He cast out demons by the Spirit of God. Hebrews 9:14 says that He offered Himself to God on the cross through the eternal Spirit. This shows that when Christ was in the flesh, He was also in resurrection.

Christ did everything in resurrection. In John 5:19 and 30 He said that He did not do anything from Himself. Instead, He lived by the One who sent Him (John 6:57a). This is resurrection. In John 14:10 the Lord Jesus said, "The words that I say to you I do not speak from Myself, but the Father who abides in Me does His works." The One who works when the Son speaks is resurrection. In our crystallization-study of John we pointed out that not only His resurrecting of Lazarus but also everything that Christ did was the exercise of Himself as resurrection. When He was in the flesh, He had a human part of His being which was not resurrection.

Whatever is human is not resurrection, but whatever is divine is resurrection. He was in the flesh, and at the same time He was also in resurrection. He lived in the flesh but He did not live by the flesh. He lived by another factor, another source, that is, by the One who sent Him. The One who sent Him was the Father, who is divine. That Divine One is resurrection.

Then when Christ passed through death and entered into resurrection, He uplifted His human part into divinity. Romans 1:3 through 4 says that Christ as the seed of David in the flesh was designated the Son of God in resurrection. To designate is to uplift His human part into divinity. In resurrection He was born to be the firstborn Son of God; as the seed of David He was designated to be the Son of God. Also, through His resurrection we were regenerated, begotten of God, to be the many sons of God (1 Pet. 1:3; Rom. 8:29). In regeneration God begets gods, who are His children in His life and nature but not in His Godhead (John 1:12-13). This is because our humanity has been uplifted, resurrected. Ephesians 2:5 and 6 reveal that we were made alive and resurrected together with Christ. Resurrection means to uplift our humanity into divinity, from the level of humanity to the level of divinity.

A. The Christ in His Incarnation

1. To Bring God into Man

Resurrection means divinity. Incarnation means humanity. Christ becoming a man was His entering into the stage of incarnation by bringing divinity into humanity. This is to bring God into man, making God and man one, as one entity, one person, one God-man. This was unprecedented in human history. There was no one before Christ who was one entity of divinity and humanity.

2. To Live in Humanity to Express God

Christ lived in humanity to express God, especially to express the attributes of God in His human virtues. Although He was in humanity, He did not express humanity. He expressed divinity. He especially expressed the attributes of God. God's attributes are what God is. God is love, light, holiness, and righteousness. When these attributes were expressed in Christ's humanity, they became His human virtues.

3. To Accomplish the All-terminating and All-redeeming Death

Christ accomplished an all-terminating and an all-redeeming death to close His ministry in His incarnation. His one death terminated all negative things. Whatever God created became fallen and was terminated by Christ's death. Also, whatever was terminated by Christ's death was redeemed, so His death is all-terminating and all-redeeming. His ministry in His incarnation was closed by His death.

B. The Christ in His Resurrection

1. Entering into His Resurrection

Through His death Christ entered into His resurrection to carry out His ministry in the stage of His inclusion. Before Christ became a man, He was God and the Son of God. At that time there was nothing of humanity in Him. But when He was brought into resurrection through His death, He became all-inclusive. Now in Him there is not only divinity but also humanity. In Him there is also His death with its effectiveness and His resurrection with its power. Now Christ is not simple; He is all-inclusive. Through His death He entered into His resurrection to carry out His ministry in another stage, the stage of inclusion. This is the stage of Christ as the life-giving Spirit (1 Cor. 15:45b).

2. Through All the Believers in Him as His Body

Christ carries out His ministry in the stage of His inclusion through all the believers in Him as His Body to accomplish God's eternal economy. Many use the term *the great commission,* but they do not see that the great commission of Christ is to carry out God's eternal economy. Most think that the great commission is just to save sinners, to carry out soul-winning. Soul-winning is the meaning of their great commission. But the great commission to us revealed in the Bible is not soul-winning, to save sinners, but to carry out God's eternal economy. The goal of this eternal economy is the New Jerusalem, which is a divine-human constitution of the processed and consummated Triune God with His redeemed, regenerated, transformed, and glorified elect.

II. THE COMMISSION OF CHRIST

A. Preparing the Apostles to Carry Out His Heavenly Ministry

After Christ entered into His resurrection from the stage of His incarnation into the stage of His inclusion, He remained among His apostles for forty days to prepare them for carrying out His heavenly ministry in His resurrection (Acts 1:2-3).

B. Giving Them His Great Commission

At the close of His forty days' preparation of the apostles, He gave them His great commission.

C. With All Authority in Heaven and on Earth Given to Him

This commission was given by Christ as the One who had been given all authority in heaven and on earth (Matt. 28:18).

D. Receiving the Great Commission as Disciples

We may think that Christ's great commission was given only to the eleven apostles and not to us. But the eleven apostles received the great commission of Christ not only as apostles but also as disciples (Matt. 28:16). When the apostles received this great commission, they were not in their status as apostles. They were in their status as disciples, which is our status. We do not have the apostolic status, but we do have the disciples' status. As disciples, we are qualified to receive Christ's great commission.

1. To Disciple the Nations

The great commission the Lord gave us is for us to disciple

the nations and teach them the teachings of Christ (Matt. 28:19-20). I have been under this discipling for about seventy years, and I am still being discipled by the Lord.

2. To Proclaim the Gospel to All the Creation

In Mark 16:15 the Lord said, "Go into all the world and proclaim the gospel to all the creation." Colossians 1:20 says that Christ reconciled all things to Himself through His death. All things, whether on earth or in the heavens, were reconciled to God, and the gospel should be proclaimed to all creation under heaven (Col. 1:23).

3. To Proclaim Repentance for Forgiveness of Sins

Christ commissioned us to proclaim repentance for forgiveness of sins (Luke 24:47). We must have the proper experience of this if we are going to proclaim it. Everyone who is seeking after the Lord needs to have a full repentance and make a thorough confession of his sins to the Lord. In 1935 Brother Nee was in my hometown holding a conference on living Christ as our victorious life. One day during that conference, I went to the meeting hall when no one was there to spend some time with the Lord. I had a thorough repentance and made a thorough confession of my sins to the Lord for more than two hours. After that confession, I felt that I was fully released and buoyant. If we do not confess our past sins to receive the cleansing of the Lord's blood with His forgiveness, we will be heavily burdened. The way to be released from this burden is to make a thorough confession of our sins to the Lord. When we experience such a repentance for the forgiveness of our sins, we will be able to effectively proclaim this to others.

4. To Witness a Resurrected Christ

The Lord has also charged us to witness a resurrected Christ appointed by God to be the Lord and Christ (Messiah), the anointed One of God, and to be the Ruler and Savior (Acts 2:32-36; 5:30-32).

5. *To Magnify Christ*

To witness Christ is to magnify Christ, to display Christ (Acts 22:15). When people saw Paul, they saw Christ. Paul said that it was no longer he who lived, but it was Christ who lived in him (Gal. 2:20a). To him to live was Christ (Phil. 1:21a). When Paul lived, he was Christ. Our witnessing is to witness that we are the very Christ whom we minister to others. When we are living Christ, all the negative things are gone and all that people see is Christ. This is a life lived in humanity but expressing a divine Christ. This is to live Christ, to magnify Christ, to display Christ, to show people Christ.

6. *To Save and Gather In All God's Chosen People*

The Lord commissioned the disciples to save and gather in all God's chosen people from Jerusalem through Judea and Samaria and unto the uttermost part of the earth—all the world, all the nations (Acts 1:8; Mark 16:15; Luke 24:47). Today's Jerusalem to us is all of our close acquaintances. We have to save them, gather them in, and reap them. Those who are laboring for the Lord's interests in Russia are Christ's witnesses at the uttermost part of the earth. The object of our commission is eventually to gain all the nations, the whole earth.

To carry out the great commission of Christ in resurrection, we must live the divine life in our human life. We live in the human life, but we do not live the human life. Instead, we live the divine life in the human life. Resurrection means that our natural life has been crucified, has been conformed to the death of Christ. Now we live in the human life, but we do not live the human life. We live the divine life, and this divine life is resurrection. Resurrection means that our natural life is crucified. We have to deny ourselves, to have our natural man, our human life, crucified with Christ. Then we let Christ live in us to be the divine life. Resurrection means not to live our natural life but to live the divine life. Our humanity is then uplifted to the divine life through and in resurrection.

THE VITAL GROUPS

MESSAGE SIX

SHEPHERDING AND TEACHING—
THE OBLIGATION OF THE VITAL GROUPS

THE BASIC WAY ORDAINED BY GOD
IN THE BUILDING UP OF THE BODY OF CHRIST
TO CONSUMMATE HIS ETERNAL GOAL—
THE NEW JERUSALEM

(1)

OUTLINE

I. In Christ's ministry for carrying out God's eternal economy:
   A. Shepherding outwardly:
      1. Seeking the lost sheep for His rejoicing and the joy in heaven—Luke 15:4-7.
      2. For the reaping of God's harvest—Matt. 9:36-38.
      3. For the care of God's flock:
         a. To be the door in and the door out for God's elect—John 10:2-5.
         b. For their salvation and nourishment (the pasture) that they may have His life and have it abundantly through His giving up of His human life as the good Shepherd—John 10:9-15, 17-18.
         c. Flocking them together as one flock—one church—John 10:16.
      4. As the Chief Shepherd shepherding through the elders of the churches—1 Pet. 5:4.
      5. As the great Shepherd through whom God, based upon His redeeming blood of the eternal covenant, perfects the sheep of God, the churches, in every good work for the doing of

His will, doing in us that which is well pleasing in His sight—Heb. 13:20-21.

   6. Shepherding the sheep led astray and returned to Him, overseeing their inward condition as the Overseer of their souls (1 Pet. 2:25). This should be a part of His inward comforting of the believers as follows.

B. Comforting inwardly:

   1. Becoming the Spirit of reality as the second Comforter—John 14:16-17a; 15:26.

   2. To constitute the divine organism, the incorporation of the processed and consummated Triune God with His regenerated and transformed elect—John 14:17b-20.

C. Teaching to strengthen the shepherding and reach its goal:

   1. In Matthew:

     a. Concerning the constitution of the kingdom of the heavens—chs. 5—7.

     b. Concerning the mysteries of the kingdom—ch. 13.

     c. Concerning the manifestation of the kingdom—chs. 24—25.

   2. In John:

     a. Concerning the flowing Triune God to be the living water for the enjoyment of the believers in Christ—chs. 1—7.

     b. Concerning the mingling and the incorporation of the processed and consummated Triune God with His regenerated and transformed elect and the issues—chs. 14—17.

   3. All these divine and mystical teachings of our great Shepherd and Comforter are not only His unveiling and enlightening but also His nourishing to us for our growth and maturity in His divine life that the eternal economy of God may be consummated through us.

Shepherding and teaching are the obligation of the vital groups. If we do not do this, we owe something to the Lord, to the saints, and to all the sinners on this earth (Rom. 1:14). Shepherding and teaching are our obligation as a charge given to us by the Lord. This is the basic way ordained by God in the building up of the Body of Christ to consummate His eternal goal—the New Jerusalem.

I. IN CHRIST'S MINISTRY
FOR CARRYING OUT GOD'S ECONOMY

The Gospels reveal Christ's shepherding and teaching in His ministry for carrying out God's eternal economy.

A. Shepherding Outwardly

1. Seeking the Lost Sheep

Christ sought the lost sheep for His rejoicing and the joy in heaven (Luke 15:4-7).

2. For the Reaping of God's Harvest

Christ came as the Shepherd not just to seek the lost ones but also to reap God's harvest (Matt. 9:36-38). On the one hand, those in the vital groups should go out to seek the lost sinners; on the other hand, they should go out to reap God's harvest.

3. For the Care of God's Flock

a. To Be the Door In and the Door Out for God's Elect

Christ's shepherding was for the care of God's flock. He was the door in and the door out for God's elect (John 10:2-5). He was the door into the fold for the Old Testament saints such as Moses, Joshua, David, and Isaiah. The fold signifies the law, or Judaism as the religion of the law. When Christ came in the New Testament, He was the door out of the fold so that God's chosen people, such as Peter, John, James, and Paul, could come out to enjoy Him as the pasture. John 9 tells the story of a blind man who was healed by the Lord. Christ became his door out of the Judaism-fold.

b. For Their Salvation and Nourishment

Christ is the door to God's elect for their salvation and nourishment (the pasture) that they may have His life and have it abundantly through His giving up of His human life as the good Shepherd (John 10:9-15, 17-18). All the members of the vital groups should be like Christ. We should be the door to people for their salvation and nourishment, so that they can feed on Christ as their pasture that they may have His divine life abundantly.

c. Flocking Them Together as One Flock— One Church

In John 10:16 the Lord said, "I have other sheep, which are not of this fold; I must lead them also, and they shall hear My voice, and there shall be one flock, one Shepherd." This means that Christ was the Shepherd flocking the divided Jewish and Gentile sheep together to be one flock. Some so-called co-workers work in a divisive way. Instead of flocking the saints together, they scatter them. The proper shepherding work is to flock people together.

4. As the Chief Shepherd

Christ is the Chief Shepherd, shepherding His flock through the elders of the churches (1 Pet. 5:4). All the elders are subordinate shepherds. Christ as the Head is the Chief Shepherd. Actually, we are not the ones who are shepherding. When we shepherd, it should be Christ shepherding through us. If we shepherd people apart from Christ, this is not in resurrection but in the old creation. When Christ shepherds through us, our labor is in resurrection. Only Christ is resurrection. Whatever is divine is resurrection. All the elders have to learn to shepherd the churches not by themselves in the old creation but by Christ as the shepherding Chief in resurrection.

5. As the Great Shepherd

Christ is the great Shepherd through whom God, based upon His redeeming blood of the eternal covenant, perfects the sheep of God, the churches, in every good work for the doing of His will, doing in us that which is well pleasing in His sight (Heb. 13:20-21). This is the only place in the whole book of Hebrews which speaks of the Triune God being in us.

6. As the Overseer of the Believers' Souls

Christ shepherds the sheep led astray and returned to Him, overseeing their inward condition as the Overseer of their souls (1 Pet. 2:25). This should be a part of His inward comforting of the believers.

B. Comforting Inwardly

When the Lord's shepherding goes deeper in us, it reaches our soul to take care of our inward condition for the doing of the will of God in us. Christ as the Shepherd of our soul oversees the inward situation of our soul, which is composed of our mind, emotion, and will. We need Him to perfect our mind, adjust our emotion, and correct our will.

1. Becoming the Spirit of Reality

Christ became the Spirit of reality as the second Comforter (John 14:16-17a; 15:26). The first Comforter was Christ in the flesh, and the second Comforter is Christ as the life-giving Spirit, the Spirit of reality.

2. To Constitute the Divine Organism

Christ comforts us inwardly to constitute the divine organism, the incorporation of the processed and consummated Triune God with His regenerated and transformed elect (John 14:17b-20). As the second Comforter, Christ is the Spirit of reality who comes not only to be with us but also to be in us, the redeemed ones of God (v. 17). Then the Son in whom we believe is in the Father and we are in Him and He is in us (v. 20). These four *in*s show the Triune God incorporated with His redeemed and transformed people to be one entity.

C. Teaching to Strengthen
the Shepherding and Reach Its Goal

1. In Matthew

a. Concerning the Constitution
of the Kingdom of the Heavens

The constitution of the kingdom in Matthew 5 through 7 charges the believers of Christ, the kingdom people, to be poor in spirit (5:3), to be pure in heart (v. 8), and to have the righteousness which exceeds that of the scribes and Pharisees (v. 20).

b. Concerning the Mysteries of the Kingdom

The Lord's teaching concerning the mysteries of the kingdom is in Matthew 13. This chapter reveals that we need to be the good ground to grow Christ and be transformed into the great pearl (vv. 23, 45-46).

c. Concerning the Manifestation of the Kingdom

Matthew 24 and 25 reveal the manifestation of the kingdom of the heavens and speak of the overcoming believers being taken in the first rapture, being rewarded as faithful servants of the Lord, and entering into the kingdom as the wise virgins.

2. In John

a. Concerning the Flowing Triune God

John 1 through 7 is concerning the flowing Triune God to be the living water for the enjoyment of the believers in Christ. We enjoy the Triune God with the Father as the fountain, the Son as the spring, and the Spirit as the river flowing into the totality of the eternal life, the New Jerusalem (4:14b).

b. Concerning the Mingling and the Incorporation
of the Processed and Consummated Triune God with
His Regenerated and Transformed Elect and the Issues

John 14 through 17 is concerning the mingling and the incorporation of the processed and consummated Triune God with His regenerated and transformed elect and the issues. The issues of this mingling and incorporation are the believers' participating in the Father's house, in the Son's vine, and in the Spirit's child to be in the oneness of the Body of Christ incorporated with the oneness of the Triune God.

3. Christ's Divine and Mystical Teachings Nourishing Us for Our Growth and Maturity in His Divine Life

All these divine and mystical teachings of our great Shepherd and Comforter are not only His unveiling and enlightening but also His nourishing to us for our growth and maturity in His divine life that the eternal economy of God may be consummated through us.

Christ came to seek the sinners that they might have His life and have it abundantly, so we should not go out to reach people in a shallow and empty way. We should go out full of the divine life so that people may have Christ's life through us. We must be filled to the brim with Christ's life so that His life flows out of us to be dispensed into others. We need to be saturated and soaked with Christ inwardly and outwardly. In this sense, we become Christ and the eternal life because we have drunk of God as the fountain, emerging into the spring, and gushing up into a river of life to flow out of our innermost being.

We also need to teach the divine truths to people to strengthen our shepherding and reach its goal. We may share with a theological professor concerning the four *in*s in John 14:17-20. Our going out as Christ to give people life and truth will attract and convince them. We need to be discipled to be such a Christ. On the one hand, we should shepherd people by dispensing the divine life into them. On the other hand, we should teach them the divine truths in the divine, mystical realm. This is my burden.

If we practice these things, there will be a real revival in the Lord's recovery. We must be shepherds with the loving and forgiving heart of our Father God in His divinity and the shepherding and finding spirit of our Savior Christ in His humanity. We also must have the heavenly vision of all the divine and mystical teachings of Christ. Shepherding and teaching are the obligation of the vital groups and the basic way ordained by God to build up the Body of Christ consummating the New Jerusalem.

THE VITAL GROUPS

SHEPHERDING AND TEACHING—
THE OBLIGATION OF THE VITAL GROUPS

THE BASIC WAY ORDAINED BY GOD
IN THE BUILDING UP OF THE BODY OF CHRIST
TO CONSUMMATE HIS ETERNAL GOAL—
THE NEW JERUSALEM

(2)

OUTLINE

II. In the gifts (among the gifted persons) given by Christ the ascended Head to the churches for the building up of His Body, the essential functions are:

A. Shepherding:

1. Among the four kinds of gifted persons, the ministry of the first three, that is, of the apostles, prophets, and evangelists, depends upon shepherding. This is confirmed by the Lord's charge to Peter in John 21:15-17.

2. Contacting and taking care of others, sinners and believers, as the apostle Paul, the top apostle, did in contacting people and taking care of people's need—2 Cor. 1:23—2:14; 11:28-29.

B. Teaching:

1. The apostle Paul taught in his personal visits to the churches—1 Cor. 4:17b; 7:17b.

2. Paul also wrote fourteen Epistles to the churches and individuals concerning God's eternal economy with Christ as its centrality and universality and the Body of Christ as its central line to consummate the New Jerusalem.

III. In the eldership:
 A. In addition to the shepherding by the main func-
    tion of the gifted persons, Christ as the Head of
    the church also charged the apostles to appoint
    elders (overseers) in all the local churches to carry
    out His shepherding of His flock—1 Tim. 3:1-7;
    5:17a.
 B. The obligation of the elders in the churches is:
    1. Shepherding (1 Pet. 5:2a), as Christ did and as
       the gifted persons do.
    2. Teaching to strengthen the shepherding and
       carry out its goal (1 Tim. 3:2b; 5:17b) according
       to what Christ taught in the four Gospels and
       what the gifted persons taught in the Epistles.
 C. The elders shepherding the churches by taking
    the lead should not lord it over them, God's allot-
    ments to the elders, but should become patterns of
    God's flock—1 Tim. 5:17; 1 Pet. 5:2-3:
    1. Girding themselves with humility to serve the
       saints—1 Pet. 5:5-6; cf. 2 Cor. 4:5; Matt. 20:26-28;
       3 John 9-11.
    2. Their willing and faithful shepherding will be
       rewarded with the unfading crown of glory at
       the manifestation of the Chief Shepherd—
       1 Pet. 5:4.

In the previous message we saw that shepherding and teaching are in Christ's ministry for carrying out God's eternal economy. In this message we want to see the shepherding and teaching in the gifted persons and in the eldership.

II. IN THE GIFTS

Shepherding and teaching are the essential functions in the gifts (among the gifted persons) given by Christ the ascended Head to the churches for the building up of His Body.

A. Shepherding

1. The Ministry of the Apostles, Prophets, and Evangelists Depending upon Shepherding

Among the four kinds of gifted persons, the ministry of the first three, that is, of the apostles, prophets, and evangelists, depends upon shepherding. This is confirmed by the Lord's charge to Peter in John 21:15-17. The functions of these leading gifted persons depend upon shepherding. Without shepherding, the apostles, prophets, and evangelists cannot function.

The preaching of the gospel is the top shepherding of sinners. The Lord Jesus was the first New Testament preacher. John the Baptist was the forerunner. The first gospel preacher, Christ, carried out His ministry by shepherding. He went to Jericho just to visit one person, a chief tax collector (Luke 19:1-10). He did not go there to hold a big gospel campaign with thousands of people. His desire was to preach the gospel to gain one person, and His preaching was a shepherding.

John 4 says that while the Lord was on His way to Galilee, "He had to pass through Samaria" (v. 4). He detoured from the main way to Sychar, near Jacob's well, in order to contact a sinful Samaritan woman, who previously had five husbands. The Lord foreknew that she would come to the well of Jacob. The well of Jacob is a type of Christ, who is the spring of water gushing up into eternal life (v. 14b). We have to learn of the Lord's pattern in purposely detouring to Sychar to gain only one person.

To spend three years to gain one person is worthwhile. If you spend three years to visit one person continually, you will gain him. After twelve years you will have four new ones following you to the church meetings. If one hundred saints in a local church practice this, their number can be increased to five hundred after twelve years. In this light we need to consider how much increase we have had in our locality in the past twelve years. Where is the increase among us? The proper increase is due to the gospel shepherding, and shepherding means that we have to go and visit people. Christ visited the sinners by coming down from heaven to earth to find the lost sheep, one by one. We have to learn of Him.

John 21 is a chapter on shepherding. In our crystallization-study of the Gospel of John we saw that this chapter is not merely an appendix but also the completion and consummation of the Gospel of John, a book on Christ being God coming to be our life. The writer of this Gospel spent twenty chapters to unveil such a Christ. Eventually, such a book has a conclusion on shepherding. If we do not know what shepherding is, the entire Gospel of John will be in vain to us. It is only when we shepherd others that we can know John in an intrinsic way. Shepherding is the key to the Gospel of John.

John 21:15 says, "Jesus said to Simon Peter, Simon, son of John, do you love Me more than these? He said to Him, Yes, Lord, You know that I love You." Peter said, "Lord, You know," because he had denied the Lord three times. He lost his natural confidence in his love toward the Lord. In restoring Peter's love toward Him, the Lord charged him to shepherd and feed His sheep.

In his first Epistle, Peter spoke in 2:25 of Christ being the Shepherd and Overseer of our soul, our inner being and real person. Then in 5:1-2 he told the elders that their obligation is to shepherd God's flock according to God. *According to God* means that we must live God. We must have God on hand. We have God in our understanding, in our theology, and in our teaching, but we may not live God when we are shepherding people. When we are one with God, we become God. Then we have God and are God in our shepherding of others. To shepherd according to God is to shepherd according to what God is in His attributes. God is love, light, holiness, and right-eousness. *According to God* is at least according to these four attributes of God. We must shepherd the young ones, the weak ones, and the backsliding ones according to these four attributes. Then we will be good shepherds.

Without shepherding, there is no way for us to minister life to others. John is the Gospel of life. If we want to enjoy life and minister life to others, we must shepherd them. The real ministering of life is shepherding by visiting and contacting people.

2. The Pattern of the Apostle Paul in Shepherding

We need to contact and take care of others, sinners and believers, as the apostle Paul, the top apostle, did in contacting people and taking care of people's need (2 Cor. 1:23—2:14). In 2 Corinthians 11:28-29 Paul said, "Apart from the things which have not been mentioned, there is this: the crowd of cares pressing upon me daily, the anxious concern for all the churches. Who is weak, and I am not weak? Who is stumbled, and I myself do not burn?" This unveils the care of a proper shepherd.

Our attitude may be that everyone is weak but we are not weak. We may have the feeling that we are strong ones. In 1 Corinthians 9:22 Paul said, "To the weak I became weak that I might gain the weak." This means that we should come down to the weak one's level. To a sick person we come down to the level of a sick person. This is the way to shepherd people by visiting them. Paul also said, "Who is stumbled, and I myself do not burn?" This is to burn in sorrow and indignation over the cause of the stumbling of all the fallen ones. This shows the pattern of Paul as a good shepherd, taking care of God's flock.

Acts 20 says that while Paul was on his way to Jerusalem, he sent word to Ephesus and called for the elders of the church. He told them that they should shepherd God's flock, which God purchased with His own blood (v. 28). The shepherding of God's flock was on Paul's heart. Many think that Paul was a great apostle doing a great work as a great career. But Paul considered what he did as shepherding the flock of God. We have to be revolutionized in our logic and consideration. We should not think that we are going to do a great work for Christ like certain spiritual giants. These so-called giants actually did not accomplish much for God's interest. Instead, they only made a name for themselves with little result for the building up of the Body of Christ.

B. Teaching

1. Paul's Teaching in His Personal Visits to the Churches

The apostle Paul taught in his personal visits to the churches (1 Cor. 4:17b; 7:17b).

2. Paul's Writing Fourteen Epistles

Paul also wrote fourteen Epistles to the churches and individuals concerning God's eternal economy with Christ as its centrality and universality and the Body of Christ as its central line to consummate the New Jerusalem. What Paul taught was the same as what the Lord Jesus taught. Many teachings today are in the realm of ethics. They are not up to the standard of what Christ and Paul taught. Both Christ and Paul taught the contents of God's eternal economy. In our vital groups we have to learn to teach these things.

If we are going to teach the Gospel of Matthew, we need to know its three main sections: the constitution of the kingdom (chs. 5—7), the mysteries of the kingdom (ch. 13), and the manifestation of the kingdom (chs. 24—25). In the constitution of the kingdom, we have to be poor in spirit and pure in heart and to have a righteousness which exceeds that of the Pharisees. If we teach the mysteries of the kingdom, we have to stress that we need to be the good ground, into which Christ sows Himself as the seed. Today we have to grow Christ and be transformed into a great pearl. We should also teach from John that God is the flowing God. The Father is the fountain emerging to be the spring in the Son and gushing up to be the river as the Spirit unto a great consummation, the New Jerusalem. These are the teachings we should learn and minister to others. When we teach these things, people will be surprised and attracted. They will also receive the supply and the ministry of life.

III. IN THE ELDERSHIP

A. Carrying Out His Shepherding of His Flock

In addition to the shepherding by the main function of the gifted persons, Christ as the Head of the church also charged the apostles to appoint elders (overseers) in all the local churches to carry out His shepherding of His flock (1 Tim. 3:1-7; 5:17a). The Head of the church gave many gifted persons to function in shepherding for the building up of His Body, but the Body is manifested in the local churches. The Body is universal and abstract, but the churches are located and substantial. In the local churches, the elders as the local shepherds are needed. The local shepherds are more practical. Christ as the Head of the church charged the apostles, the universal shepherds, to appoint some local elders to take care of the located churches.

B. The Obligation of the Elders in the Churches

1. Shepherding

The obligation of the elders in the churches is to shepherd (1 Pet. 5:2a), as Christ did and as the gifted persons do.

2. Teaching

The elders are also obligated to teach to strengthen the shepherding and carry out its goal (1 Tim. 3:2b; 5:17b) according to what Christ taught in the four Gospels and what the gifted persons taught in the Epistles. First Timothy 3:2 says that the elders must be apt to teach. This means that teaching is their habit. Some elders have a quiet disposition. These ones especially must deny themselves to be apt to teach, and to be apt to teach is to be apt to talk. This is not to talk about vain things but about the truths of God's economy. We have to be equipped by the Lord's grace to speak for Him. We should speak the high peaks of the truth of God's eternal economy. Paul also said in 1 Timothy 5:17 that the elders who labor in the word and teaching are worthy of double honor. In 1 Timothy 1:3-4 Paul charged Timothy to remain in Ephesus to tell certain ones not to teach anything different from God's economy. He also charged the Corinthians to speak the same thing so that there would be no divisions among them (1 Cor. 1:10). We all should speak the same thing—God's economy.

C. Becoming Patterns of God's Flock

The elders shepherding the churches by taking the lead should not lord it over them, God's allotments to the elders, but should become patterns of God's flock (1 Tim. 5:17; 1 Pet. 5:2-3). The churches have been allotted to the elders, entrusted to them by God for their care. They have to shepherd the saints, not lord it over them.

1. Girding Themselves with Humility

The elders should gird themselves with humility to serve the saints (1 Pet. 5:5-6). In 2 Corinthians 4:5 Paul said, "For we do not preach ourselves but Christ Jesus as Lord, and ourselves as your slaves for Jesus' sake." The co-workers and the elders are slaves. Matthew 20:26-27 says, "Whoever wants to become great among you shall be your servant, and whoever wants to be first among you shall be your slave." There is a negative illustration in 3 John 9-11: "I wrote something to the church; but Diotrephes, who loves to be first among them, does not receive us. For this reason, if I come, I will bring to remembrance his works which he does, babbling against us with evil words; and not being satisfied with these, neither does he himself receive the brothers, and those intending to do so he forbids and casts out of the church. Beloved, do not imitate the evil, but the good. He who does good is of God; he who does evil has not seen God." The self-exalting and domineering Diotrephes is an evil pattern.

2. Being Rewarded with the Unfading Crown of Glory

The elders' willing and faithful shepherding will be

rewarded with the unfading crown of glory at the manifestation of the Chief Shepherd (1 Pet. 5:4). Christ as the Chief Shepherd is taking care of the shepherding of His churches. When He comes back, He will reward the faithful ones who cooperated with Him.

THE VITAL GROUPS

MESSAGE EIGHT

LOVE PREVAILS

OUTLINE

I. God is love; we love because He first loved us—1 John 4:8, 19.

II. God's predestination of us unto the divine sonship was motivated by the divine love—Eph. 1:4-5.

III. God's giving of His only begotten Son to us that we may be saved from perdition judicially through His death and have the eternal life organically in His resurrection was motivated by the divine love—John 3:16; 1 John 4:9-10.

IV. God's love is the source of the grace of Christ dispensed to us through the fellowship of the Spirit—2 Cor. 13:14.

V. God's love motivates us, His children, to love our enemies that we may be perfect as He is; He loves the fallen human race, who became His enemies, by causing His sun (signifying Christ) to rise on the evil and the good indiscriminately and sending rain (signifying the Spirit) on the just and the unjust equally; thus, we may become the sons of the heavenly Father who are sanctified from the tax collectors and the Gentiles—Matt. 5:43-48.

VI. Love builds up—1 Cor. 8:1b.

VII. Love is not jealous, is not provoked, does not take account of evil, covers all things, endures all things, never falls away, and is the greatest—1 Cor. 13:4-8, 13.

VIII. Love is the conclusion of all spiritual virtues and the factor of fruit-bearing that supplies us bountifully with the rich entrance into the kingdom of Christ—2 Pet. 1:5-11.

    IX. The Body of Christ builds itself up in love—Eph. 4:16.

    X. The spirit that God gives us is of love; hence, it is of power and of sobermindedness—2 Tim. 1:7.

    XI. He who does not love abides in death—1 John 3:14b.

    XII. Pursue love while you desire spiritual gifts—1 Cor. 14:1.

    XIII. To overcome the degradation of the church we need to pursue love with those who seek the Lord out of a pure heart—2 Tim. 2:22.

    XIV. Loving one another is a sign that we belong to Christ—John 13:34-35.

    XV. The love of God makes us more than conquerors over our circumstantial situations—Rom. 8:35-39.

    XVI. Love is the most excellent way—1 Cor. 12:31b.

In the previous two messages we saw that shepherding and teaching are the obligation of the vital groups. In this message we want to see that love prevails. Regardless of how much we shepherd and teach others, without love everything is in vain. First Corinthians 13 is a chapter covering one unique thing, that is, love. This chapter tells us that even if we prophesy in the highest way and give everything for others, without love they mean nothing (vv. 2-3). Both shepherding and teaching need love, not our natural love but His divine love.

I. GOD BEING LOVE

We are God's species because we have been born of Him to have His life and nature (John 1:12-13). We have been regenerated to be God's species, God's kind, and God is love. Since we become God in His life and nature, we also should be love. This means that we do not merely love others but that we are love itself. As His species we should be love because He is love. Whoever is love is God's species, God's kind.

God is love; we love because He first loved us (1 John 4:8, 19). God does not want us to love with our natural love but with Him as our love. God created man in His image (Gen. 1:26), which means that He created man according to what He is. God's image is what God is, and His attributes are what He is. According to the revelation in the holy Scriptures, God's first attribute is love. God created man according to His attributes, the first of which is love. Although created man does not have the reality of love, there is something in his created being that wants to love others. Even fallen man has the desire to love within him. But that is just a human virtue, the very expression of the divine attribute of love. When we were regenerated, God infused us with Himself as love. We love Him because He first loved us. He initiated this love.

II. GOD'S PREDESTINATION OF US UNTO THE DIVINE SONSHIP

God's predestination of us unto the divine sonship was motivated by the divine love. Ephesians 1:4-5 says that God

chose us in Christ before the foundation of the world "to be
holy and without blemish before Him in love, predestinating
us unto sonship." The phrase *in love* can be joined with the
phrase *predestinating us unto sonship.* God predestinated us
unto sonship in love. John 3:16 says that God so loved the
world. He loved us before the foundation of the world.

III. GOD'S GIVING OF HIS ONLY BEGOTTEN SON TO US BEING MOTIVATED BY THE DIVINE LOVE

God's giving of His only begotten Son to us that we may be
saved from perdition judicially through His death and have
the eternal life organically in His resurrection was motivated
by the divine love (John 3:16; 1 John 4:9-10). John 3:16 is
strengthened by two verses from John's first Epistle—4:9
and 10. First John 4:10 says that God sent His Son to us as a
propitiation for our sins. This is judicial through His death.
Verse 9 says that God sent His Son to us that we may have
life and live through Him. This is organic in His resurrection.
John 3:16 should be read with 1 John 4:9-10.

IV. GOD'S LOVE BEING THE SOURCE

God's love is the source of the grace of Christ dispensed to
us through the fellowship of the Spirit (2 Cor. 13:14). This is
for us to enjoy the processed and consummated Triune God.

V. GOD'S LOVE MOTIVATING US TO LOVE OUR ENEMIES

God's love motivates us, His children, to love our enemies
that we may be perfect as He is; He loves the fallen human
race, who became His enemies, by causing His sun (signifying
Christ) to rise on the evil and the good indiscriminately and
sending rain (signifying the Spirit) on the just and the unjust
equally; thus, we may become the sons of the heavenly Father
who are sanctified from the tax collectors and the Gentiles
(Matt. 5:43-48). The entire human race became His enemies,
but God still loves the human race. If God sent Christ to us
with discrimination, we would be disqualified from receiving
His salvation. He causes His sun to rise first on the evil and
then on the good without discrimination.

We should be like God in our love for others. The tax

collectors love only those who love them. The Lord said, "If you love those who love you, what reward do you have? Do not even the tax collectors do the same?" (v. 46). If we love only those who love us, we are of the same species as the tax collectors. But we are of the super, divine species, so we love the evil ones, our enemies, as well as the good ones. This shows how God as love prevails.

The vital groups should be groups that are prevailing. A proof that our vital group is prevailing is that we love people without any discrimination. Some Christian co-workers may feel that we should let certain persons suffer eternal perdition. They may say that they would not love certain persons, such as bank robbers. But while Christ was being crucified on the cross, two robbers were crucified with Him (Matt. 27:38). One of them said, "Jesus, remember me when You come into Your kingdom" (Luke 23:42). Jesus said to him, "Truly I say to you, Today you shall be with Me in Paradise" (v. 43). The first one saved by Christ through His crucifixion was not a gentleman, but a criminal, a robber, sentenced to death. This is very meaningful.

VI. LOVE BUILDS UP

First Corinthians 8:1b says, "Knowledge puffs up, but love builds up." Teaching without love may puff us up. We may listen to the messages of the ministry and become puffed up with mere knowledge. This does not build up. Love builds up.

VII. LOVE BEING THE GREATEST

Love is not jealous, is not provoked, does not take account of evil, covers all things, endures all things, never falls away, and is the greatest (1 Cor. 13:4-8, 13). Jealousy is in our nature. When a new child is born in a family, the other child may become jealous. Jealousy is also present in the church life. One sister may be jealous of another sister because she receives many "amens" from the saints when she prays or prophesies. Some brothers may be jealous when they see that another brother has been appointed into the eldership. After being in the church life for over sixty years, I can testify that one of the hardest things is to appoint the elders. We realize that if we appoint a certain brother, another brother whom we do not feel to appoint may be stumbled because of jealousy. If a certain sister is asked to take the lead in a sisters' house, the others may become jealous, but love is not jealous. Also, love is not provoked. People are easily provoked because of the shortage of love. Regardless of how much we are rebuked, we will not be provoked if we are filled with the divine love. Love does not take account of evil. We have to confess that we have taken account of other people's evil. Some wives have a record, an account, of their husband's failures and defects. This record may not be written but it is in their mind. They are taking account of their husband's evil.

The elders need to realize that in their shepherding, they have to cover others' sins, not to take account of others' evils. Love covers all things, not only the good things but also the bad things. Whoever uncovers the defects, shortcomings, and sins of the members of the church is disqualified from the eldership. Our uncovering of the members under our eldership, our shepherding, annuls our qualification. Love also endures all things and never falls away. First Corinthians 13 concludes by saying, "Now there abide faith, hope, love, these three; and the greatest of these is love."

VIII. LOVE BEING THE CONCLUSION OF ALL SPIRITUAL VIRTUES AND THE FACTOR OF FRUIT-BEARING

Love is the conclusion of all spiritual virtues and the factor of fruit-bearing that supplies us bountifully with the rich entrance into the kingdom of Christ (2 Pet. 1:5-11).

IX. THE BODY BUILDING ITSELF UP IN LOVE

The Body of Christ builds itself up in love (Eph. 4:16). The phrase *in love* is used repeatedly in the book of Ephesians (1:4; 3:17; 4:2, 15-16; 5:2). God predestinated us unto sonship before the foundation of the world in love, and the Body of Christ builds itself up in love. The growth in life is in love. In the last few years we have appreciated the Lord's showing us the high peak of the divine revelation. My concern is that although we may talk about the truths of the high peak, love is absent among us. If this is the case, we are puffed up, not built up. The Body of Christ builds itself up in love.

X. THE SPIRIT THAT GOD GIVES US BEING OF LOVE

The spirit that God has given us is our human spirit regenerated and indwelt by the Holy Spirit. This spirit is a spirit of love; hence, it is of power and of sobermindedness (2 Tim. 1:7). We may think that we are very powerful and sober, but our spirit is not of love. We talk to people in a way that is full of power and sobermindedness, but our talk threatens them.

Paul said that we need to fan our gift into flame (v. 6). The main gift which God has given us is our regenerated human spirit with His Spirit, His life, and His nature. We must fan this gift into flame. This means that we have to stir up our spirit so that our spirit will be burning. Romans 12:11 says that we should be burning in spirit. If our spirit is not a spirit of love, our fanning it into flame will burn the whole recovery in a negative way. We must have a burning spirit of love, not a burning spirit of authority which damages. Whatever is mentioned in 2 Timothy is a requirement for us to face the degradation of the church. How can we overcome the degradation of the church? We must have a burning human spirit of love. Under today's degradation of the church, we all need a spirit of love fanned into flame to be burning in spirit. Love prevails in this way.

According to my observation throughout the years, most of the co-workers have a human spirit of "power" but not of love. We need a spirit of love to conquer the degradation of today's church. We should not say or do anything to threaten people. Instead we should always say and do things with a spirit of love, which has been fanned into flame. This is what the recovery needs.

XI. THE ONE WHO DOES NOT LOVE ABIDING IN DEATH

First John 3:14b says that he who does not love abides in death. We may think that we are living, but we are dead because we do not love. If we do not love our brother, we abide in death and are dead, but if we do love him, we abide in life and are living.

XII. PURSUING LOVE

First Corinthians 13 speaks of love, and then chapter fourteen begins by saying that we are to pursue love while we desire spiritual gifts (v. 1). Our desiring of gifts must go along with the pursuing of love. Otherwise, the gifts will puff us up.

XIII. PURSUING LOVE WITH THOSE WHO SEEK THE LORD OUT OF A PURE HEART

To overcome the degradation of the church we need to pursue love with those who seek the Lord out of a pure heart (2 Tim. 2:22). We have to pursue love with a group of seekers of the Lord. This is a vital group.

XIV. A SIGN THAT WE BELONG TO CHRIST

Loving one another is a sign that we belong to Christ (John 13:34-35). We do not need to bear an outward sign that we are of Christ. If all the saints in the Lord's recovery love one another, the whole world will say that these people are of Christ.

XV. THE LOVE OF GOD MAKING US MORE THAN CONQUERORS

The love of God makes us more than conquerors over our circumstantial situations (Rom. 8:35-39). If we are to be more than conquerors, we need the love of Christ and of God.

XVI. LOVE BEING THE MOST EXCELLENT WAY

The end of 1 Corinthians 12 reveals that love is the most excellent way (v. 31b). How can one be an elder? Love is the most excellent way. How can one be a co-worker? Love is the most excellent way. How do we shepherd people? Love is the most excellent way. Love is the most excellent way for us to prophesy and to teach others. Love is the most excellent way for us to be anything or do anything.

Love prevails. We should love everybody, even our enemies.

If the co-workers and elders do not love the bad ones, eventually they will have nothing to do. We must be perfect as our Father is perfect (Matt. 5:48) by loving the evil ones and the good ones without any discrimination. We must be perfect as our Father because we are His sons, His species. This is most crucial. How can we be a co-worker and an elder? It is by love in every way. We must love any kind of person. The Lord Jesus said that He came to be a Physician, not for the healthy ones, but for the sick ones. The Lord said, "Those who are strong have no need of a physician, but those who are ill" (Matt. 9:12).

The church is not a police station to arrest people or a law court to judge people, but a home to raise up the believers. Parents know that the worse their children are, the more they need their raising up. If our children were angels, they would not need our parenting to raise them up. The church is a loving home to raise up the children. The church is also a hospital to heal and to recover the sick ones. Finally, the church is a school to teach and edify the unlearned ones who do not have much understanding. Because the church is a home, a hospital, and a school, the co-workers and elders should be one with the Lord to raise up, to heal, to recover, and to teach others in love.

Some of the churches, however, are police stations to arrest the sinful ones and law courts to judge them. Paul's attitude was different. He said, "Who is weak, and I am not weak?" (2 Cor. 11:29a). When the scribes and Pharisees brought an adulterous woman to the Lord, He said to them, "He who is without sin among you, let him be the first to throw a stone at her" (John 8:7). After all of them left, the Lord asked the sinful woman, "Woman, where are they? Has no one condemned you?" She said, "No one, Lord." Then Jesus said, "Neither do I condemn you" (vv. 10-11). Who is without sin? Who is perfect? Paul said, "To the weak I became weak that I might gain the weak" (1 Cor. 9:22). This is love. We should not consider that others are weak but we are not. This is not love. Love covers and builds up, so love is the most excellent way for us to be anything and to do anything for the building up of the Body of Christ.

THE VITAL GROUPS

CHRIST AS THE SON OF MAN CHERISHING US AND AS THE SON OF GOD NOURISHING US

OUTLINE

I. Illustration one:
   A. Christ as the Son of Man became the Lamb of God to take away our sin (John 1:29)—cherishing.
   B. Christ as the Son of God became the life-giving Spirit to give life to us and transform us (John 1:32-34, 42)—nourishing.

II. Illustration two:
   A. Christ as the Son of Man, in the form of the serpent, destroyed the old serpent, the source of sin, through His redeeming death (John 3:14; Heb. 2:14)—cherishing.
   B. Christ as the Son of God speaks the words of God and gives Himself as the Spirit to us not by measure that we may have the eternal life (John 3:34-36, 15-16)—nourishing.

III. Illustration three:
   A. Christ as the Son of Man (Jesus), going from Judea to Galilee, detoured into the city of Sychar, near Jacob's well, to purposely wait for the thirsty and water-seeking, immoral Samaritan woman (John 4:3-9)—cherishing.
   B. Christ as the Son of God, sent by God as a gift, gave her to drink the water of life which springs up into eternal life (John 4:10-14)—nourishing.

IV. Illustration four:
   A. Christ as the Son of Man has been designated by God to judge all the people of the world, the living and the dead (John 5:27-29; Acts 17:31;

10:42; 2 Tim. 4:1; Matt. 25:31). The judgment of
Christ has been preached to the sinners as a
cherishing to them that they might repent unto
God and receive Christ as the Son of God to
have His eternal life. The judgment in Revelation
14:6-7, as a part of the judgment of Christ, will be
declared to all the people on the earth as the eternal gospel.

  B. Christ as the Son of God was given the authority
  by God to give the eternal life to His believers
  (John 5:19-26; 17:2-3)—nourishing.

  V. Illustration five:

  A. Christ as the Son of Man would not condemn the
  sinful woman (John 8:11b)—cherishing.

  B. Christ as the Son of God (the "I Am") would free
  her from sin that she could sin no more (John
  8:11b, 24, 36)—nourishing.

  VI. Illustration six:

  A. God sent His Son as a propitiation for our sins
  in His humanity (1 John 4:10)—cherishing.

  B. God sent His Son to us that we may have life and
  live through Him in His divinity (1 John 4:9)—
  nourishing.

  This is confirmed by John 3:16: God gave us His
  only begotten Son that we who believe into Him
  may not perish through His redemption in His
  humanity (cherishing) but may have eternal life in
  His divinity (nourishing).

  VII. The illustration of the entire New Testament:

  A. Christ as the Son of Man came to redeem us from
  sin (1 Tim. 1:15)—cherishing.

  B. Christ as the Son of God came to impart the divine
  life into us abundantly (John 10:10)—nourishing.

  VIII. The illustration of Christ in eternity:

  A. As the Son of Man to be the ladder sustaining and
  maintaining the life union of all His believers with
  God (John 1:51)—cherishing.

B. As the Son of God to be the life element of the New
   Jerusalem as the divine and human constitution
   of the consummated Triune God and His glorified
   elect (Rev. 21—22)—nourishing.

The title of this message is very simple but what it conveys is inexhaustible. The content of God's entire New Testament economy is Christ as the Son of Man cherishing us and as the Son of God nourishing us.

The whole Bible is composed of both the Old and New Testaments. In the Old Testament the revelation concerning God's economy—with God, Christ, and the all-inclusive, compound, consummated Spirit—is vague without the explanation and reality of the New Testament. Mary McDonough wrote a marvelous masterpiece entitled *God's Plan of Redemption*. She and some others used the word *plan* instead of *economy*. The word *economy* is not mentioned in the Old Testament, but it is mentioned in the New Testament by the apostle Paul (Eph. 1:10; 3:9; 1 Tim. 1:4—the same Greek word is used in 1 Cor. 9:17; Eph. 3:2; Col. 1:25). God's New Testament economy covers only one person—the all-inclusive Christ. He has two statuses. One is the Son of God and the other is the Son of Man. The New Testament unveils to us the very God who is the Divine Trinity.

One day at the beginning of the new testament age, about two thousand years ago, God became a man. He came in a way to visit, to contact, His fallen creatures. Four thousand years before His first coming, He created the universe, and in the universe He created man as the very center in His image and after His likeness (Gen. 1:26). God created every creature after its kind, but He did not create man after man's kind. Man was created in the image and likeness of God, so he looks like God. Man is a copy, a photo, of God. A photo does not have a person's element or life, but it does have that person's image and likeness. One day, the Creator of the man Adam became a real man. He was conceived in a human womb and was born as a human being. Isaiah 9:6 says that a child is born to us, a son is given to us, and His name is the Mighty God and the Eternal Father.

My burden is to show you that in the New Testament the first vision is that our God suddenly became a human being, and He was born as a man in the lowest status, not into a rich man's home, but into a poor man's home. He was born in Bethlehem, but He was raised up in Nazareth. His birth at

Bethlehem was covered up by His being raised up in Nazareth. People called Him a Nazarene (Matt. 2:23). This means that He was a despised man from a despised city and a despised region. Isaiah 53 says that He was a man without any outward beauty or attraction (vv. 2-3). He was just a poor Nazarene.

Such a poor man could contact every kind of man. If He had been born as a king, few would have been able to approach Him. But He was born as a poor man, and He could and did approach every class of man, especially the poor and sick ones, such as the blind, the lepers, the sinners, and the tax collectors. He became their friend. His coming in humanity made Him a very cherishing person.

To cherish someone is to make that person happy. Sinners cannot save themselves, but Christ can take away their sins to cherish them. He came to redeem us and He died on the cross for us. He came as a Physician for the sick ones and comforted them (Matt. 9:12). He told the ones who were toiling and burdened to come to Him so that He could give them rest (11:28). He also told the thirsty ones to come to Him and drink so that they would never thirst again (John 4:10, 14; 7:37).

The Jesus who is portrayed in the four Gospels is very cherishing. He came to the world just to cherish people. All people need Him to cherish them, to make them happy, comfort them, and give them rest. If He came to us in His divine status, this would intimidate us. But even the most sinful tax collectors could sit with Him as friends, eating and talking with Him (Luke 15:1; Matt. 9:10). The scribes and Pharisees, the self-justified ones, could not bear to see Him eating with tax collectors and sinners. They did not realize that they also needed Him to be their Physician. I can testify that when I was a poor young man, Jesus came to me and cherished me. Whatever I need and want, He is. What He is meets our every need. The four Gospels reveal Christ as the cherishing Son of Man to meet the need of every fallen sinner. If you are sick of leprosy, He will cleanse you. If you are blind, He will give you sight. This is the Jesus in the four Gospels.

We have seen that the full ministry of Christ is in three stages: incarnation, inclusion, and intensification. His ministry in the first stage of incarnation was to cherish people, to draw and attract people to Him. Once He was walking in a pressing crowd, and a sick woman desperately touched the fringe of His garment and was healed (Matt. 9:20-22). Everyone needs Him, can approach Him, and can touch Him. No one who came to Him was rejected by Him. He receives all without preference or discrimination.

Once when people brought their children to the Lord, the disciples prevented them. But the Lord stopped their preventing and asked them to let the children come to Him (Matt. 19:13-15). He attracted and cherished people. His visiting was His cherishing. His death on the cross was the biggest cherishing to redeem us. Without His redemption, who could come to Him? When we heard the story of His death on the cross, our tears came down. We were attracted by Him. This is His ministry in the four Gospels.

In resurrection He was transfigured to become the life-giving Spirit, the Spirit of the bountiful supply (1 Cor. 15:45b; Phil. 1:19). This Spirit is for nourishing. As the all-inclusive Spirit from Acts through the Epistles, Christ nourishes us. This nourishing produces the church, builds up the Body of Christ, and will consummate the New Jerusalem. Because of the church's degradation, Christ's nourishing becomes sevenfold intensified in the book of Revelation to bring forth the eternal goal of God, the New Jerusalem. The totality of His nourishing will be this great universal city, which is the enlargement and expression of God. This city is the consummation of the bountiful supply of Christ as the life-giving, sevenfold intensified Spirit for nourishing us. The New Testament is composed of just two sections—cherishing and nourishing. With this revelation the entire New Testament has become a new book to me.

Now we want to look at eight illustrations in the New Testament which unveil Christ as the Son of Man cherishing us and as the Son of God nourishing us.

I. ILLUSTRATION ONE

A. Christ as the Son of Man
Becoming the Lamb of God

Christ as the Son of Man became the Lamb of God to take away our sin (John 1:29)—cherishing. If God had never become a man, He could not have become the Lamb. The One who is the Lamb is the Son of Man with humanity. It was only in humanity that God could accomplish redemption for us by dying on the cross. Our sin is the most troublesome thing to all of us, but Christ became the Lamb of God to die for us, to accomplish redemption for us, to take all our sins away. This is the greatest cherishing to us to make us happy and restful.

B. Christ as the Son of God
Becoming the Life-giving Spirit

Christ as the Son of God became the life-giving Spirit to give life to us and transform us (John 1:32-34, 42)—nourishing. As the Lamb, Christ cherished us, and as the life-giving Spirit, He nourishes us. When a child will not eat, the mother will do something to make him happy. By cherishing her child, she is able to nourish him. Our God is like a mother. First, He cherishes us, makes us happy. Then He gives us some nourishment to transform us from clay to precious stones for God's building. Without Christ's cherishing, no one would come to receive Him as the life-giving Spirit.

II. ILLUSTRATION TWO

A. Christ as the Son of Man
in the Form of the Serpent

Christ as the Son of Man, in the form of the serpent, destroyed the old serpent, the source of sin, through His redeeming death (John 3:14; Heb. 2:14)—cherishing. We were bitten by the old serpent in the garden of Eden in Genesis 3, so we have the poison, the essence, of the serpent in our being. It was not sufficient for Christ merely to become our redeeming Lamb. He also had to become in the form of the serpent. Paul in Romans 8:3 said that God sent His Son in the likeness of the flesh of sin. Christ became a serpent in form not in element. He was the reality of the brass serpent in Numbers 21 (vv. 4-9) to destroy Satan, the source of sin, through His redeeming death.

B. Christ as the Son of God Speaking the Words of God

Christ as the Son of God speaks the words of God and gives Himself as the Spirit to us not by measure that we may have the eternal life (John 3:34-36, 15-16)—nourishing. The unlimited Son of God speaks God's words and gives the Spirit to the hearers of God's word. Those who hear His word and receive the Spirit are regenerated to be His increase, His bride (vv. 29-30).

III. ILLUSTRATION THREE

A. Christ as the Son of Man Detouring into the City of Sychar

Christ as the Son of Man (Jesus), going from Judea to Galilee, detoured into the city of Sychar, near Jacob's well, to purposely wait for the thirsty and water-seeking, immoral Samaritan woman (John 4:2-9)—cherishing. The very God who became a man traveled from Judea to Galilee, and He purposely detoured to a small city to cherish an immoral woman. As the Son of Man, Christ is the detouring Savior.

B. Christ as the Son of God Giving Her to Drink the Water of Life

Christ as the Son of God, sent by God as a gift, gave her to drink the water of life which springs up into eternal life (John 4:10-14)—nourishing. First, He was the Son of Man to cherish her; then He was the Son of God to give her the living water that flows into the New Jerusalem, the totality of the eternal life.

IV. ILLUSTRATION FOUR

A. Christ as the Son of Man
Having Been Designated by God
to Judge All the People of the World

Christ as the Son of Man has been designated by God to judge all the people of the world, the living and the dead (John 5:27-29; Acts 17:31; 10:42; 2 Tim. 4:1; Matt. 25:31). The judgment of Christ has been preached to the sinners as a cherishing to them that they might repent unto God and receive Christ as the Son of God to have His eternal life. The judgment in Revelation 14:6-7, as a part of the judgment of Christ, will be declared to all the people on the earth as the eternal gospel.

B. Christ as the Son of God
Having the Authority to Give Eternal Life

Christ as the Son of God was given the authority by God to give the eternal life to His believers (John 5:19-26; 17:2-3)—nourishing. He was designated by God to be the Judge of all people for cherishing, and He was sent by God with authority to give eternal life to His believers for nourishing.

V. ILLUSTRATION FIVE

A. Christ as the Son of Man
Not Condemning the Sinful Woman

Christ as the Son of Man would not condemn the sinful woman (John 8:11b)—cherishing. This sinful woman was accused by the scribes and Pharisees, but eventually they were condemned by Christ. None of them could condemn her and they all left. The Lord said to the woman, "Has no one condemned you?" She said, "No one, Lord." Then He said, "Neither do I condemn you" (vv. 10-11). This is cherishing. None of the scribes and Pharisees could say that he was without sin. The Son of Man is the unique One without sin, so He was the only one qualified to condemn the sinful woman, but He would not do it. He came not to condemn the lost but to save them.

B. Christ as the Son of God
Freeing Her from Sin

Christ as the Son of God (the very "I Am") would free her from sin so that she could sin no more (John 8:11b, 24, 36)—nourishing. According to Exodus 3:14-15, the great "I Am" is the name of Jehovah. *Jehovah* means "I Am That I Am." The Lord told the Pharisees that if they would not believe in Him as the I Am, they would die in their sins (John 8:24). In other words, they would never be freed from their sins but would remain in their sins until they would die in them. The sinful woman, no doubt, believed in the Lord Jesus, taking Him as the very I Am, to be freed from her sins. In verse 36 the Lord said, "If therefore the Son sets you free, you shall be free indeed." Only the Son of God in His divinity can enable us to sin no more. As the Son of Man, He will not condemn us but forgive us, and as the Son of God, He will free us from sinning.

VI. ILLUSTRATION SIX

A. God Sending His Son
as a Propitiation for Our Sins

God sent His Son as a propitiation for our sins in His humanity (1 John 4:10)—cherishing. As the Son of Man, Christ came to be the sin offering to appease the situation between the sinners and God.

B. God Sending His Son
That We May Have Life

God sent His Son to us that we may have life and live through Him in His divinity (1 John 4:9)—nourishing. This is confirmed by John 3:16: God gave us His only begotten Son that we who believe into Him may not perish through His redemption in His humanity (cherishing) but may have eternal life in His divinity (nourishing). God gave His only begotten Son to redeem us in His humanity judicially so that we may have eternal life in His divinity for Him to save us organically.

VII. THE ILLUSTRATION
OF THE ENTIRE NEW TESTAMENT

A. Christ as the Son of Man Redeeming Us from Sin

Christ as the Son of Man came to redeem us from sin (1 Tim. 1:15)—cherishing. This is the first part of the New Testament.

B. Christ as the Son of God
Imparting the Divine Life into Us

Christ as the Son of God came to impart the divine life into us abundantly (John 10:10)—nourishing. This is the second part of the New Testament.

VIII. THE ILLUSTRATION OF CHRIST IN ETERNITY

A. As the Son of Man to Be the Ladder

Christ as the Son of Man will be the ladder sustaining and maintaining the life union of all His believers with God (John 1:51)—cherishing. In His humanity Christ is the standing ladder, strong and unshakable. Christ is typified by the ark within the Holy of Holies, which was built with acacia wood overlaid with gold. The wood signifies His humanity and the gold signifies His divinity. According to the revelation of the entire Bible, Christ has two natures. His human nature is the standing part and His divine nature is the overlaying part. This is why Christ in His humanity is the standing ladder. He is strong in humanity to stand in an uplifted way, not a level way, to bring heaven to earth and to join earth to heaven. This is to bring God into man and to bring man into God.

B. As the Son of God to Be the Life Element

As the Son of God, Christ will be the life element of the New Jerusalem as the divine and human constitution of the consummated Triune God and His glorified elect (Rev. 21—22)—nourishing.

THE VITAL GROUPS

CHERISHING PEOPLE IN THE HUMANITY OF JESUS

OUTLINE

I. The humanity of Jesus is His human life in resurrection.

II. The humanity of the new man of the believers in God's new creation is also in resurrection—Eph. 4:23-24.

III. The first way of the members of the vital group to contact people is by cherishing them.

IV. To cherish people is to make them happy, to comfort them, to make them feel that you are pleasant to them, easy to be contacted in everything and in every way.

V. Not by your natural man, but by your regenerated man that has been conformed to the death of Christ.

VI. The model of Jesus in cherishing people in His humanity:

A. In the Gospel of Matthew:

1. As the King of the kingdom of the heavens in His humanity, Christ came to cherish people by shining over them as the great light and by preaching the kingdom of the heavens as the gospel by charging them to repent—4:12-17.

2. As the human King of the kingdom of the heavens, Christ cherished the kingdom-seekers by blessing them with a ninefold blessing—5:1-12.

3. When the disciples asked Him to dismiss the crowd to buy food for themselves, He, being moved with compassion for the crowd, told the disciples to give what they had to the people for them to eat that He might nourish the five

thousand with five loaves and two fish, having a leftover of twelve baskets—14:14-21.

4. He did the same thing in 15:32-38.

5. When His disciples rejected people bringing their children to Him, He stopped their preventing and asked them to bring the children to Him, and He cherished the parents by laying His hands on their children—19:13-15.

B. In the Gospel of Luke:

1. Christ as the Man-Savior came to a synagogue in Nazareth and read a portion from Isaiah that says, "The Spirit of the Lord is upon Me, because He has anointed Me to announce the gospel to the poor; He has sent Me to proclaim release to the captives, and recovery of sight to the blind, to send away in release those who are oppressed, to proclaim the acceptable year of the Lord, the year of jubilee," to cherish people with the words of grace proceeding out of His mouth—4:16-22.

2. Christ as the Son of Man came to eat and drink with the tax collectors and sinners, even as their friend, to cherish them that they might be nourished by Him with His redemption and salvation—7:34.

3. Christ as the Son of Man went to Jericho, passed by the tree from which Zaccheus was expecting to see Him, and looked up and said to him, "Zaccheus, hurry and come down, for today I must stay in your house," in order to cherish him that He might nourish him with His salvation—19:1-10.

C. In the Gospel of John:

1. When Christ as the God-Savior was recognized by Nathanael as the Son of God, He answered him that he would see heaven opened and the angels of God ascending and descending on Him as the Son of Man, like the heavenly ladder seen by Jacob in his dream, as a kind

of cherishing to encourage Nathanael to follow
Him that he might participate in His nourishment with all the divine benefits as revealed in
the entire Gospel of John—1:45-51.

2. When Christ as the God-Savior wanted to save
an immoral woman of Samaria, He had to
travel from Judea to Galilee through Samaria
and detoured from the main way of Samaria to
the city of Sychar, and He waited at the well of
Jacob, near Sychar, for His object to come that
He might cherish her by asking her to give Him
something to drink so that He might nourish
her with the water of life, which is the flowing
Triune God Himself—4:1-14.

3. When none of the accusing Pharisees could
condemn the adulterous woman, Christ as the
God-Savior, in His humanity, said to her, "Neither do I condemn you," to cherish her that He,
as the great I Am, might nourish her with the
freedom from sin and enable her to "sin no
more"—8:3-11, 24, 34-36.

In this message we do not want to stress the Lord's cherishing us but our cherishing others. The model of Jesus as the Son of Man cherishing people needs to be reproduced in us so that we also will cherish others in His humanity.

I. THE HUMANITY OF JESUS
IS HIS HUMAN LIFE IN RESURRECTION

When we go out to contact people, we must be persons living a human life in resurrection. In John 11:25 the Lord told Martha, "I am the resurrection." Martha complained to the Lord that if He had come sooner, her brother would not have died. But the Lord revealed that resurrection is not a matter of time but a matter of His person, because He is the resurrection.

The main vision of Jesus in the four Gospels, especially in the Synoptic Gospels, Matthew, Mark, and Luke, is that He lived a life that was human but in resurrection. Jesus was not a man living a natural life. He always put His humanity aside. He was in His humanity, yet He did not live a life of His humanity. Every day while He was on the earth, Jesus was in the flesh, but that flesh was in resurrection. Apparently, He was a Nazarene, a natural Galilean. He was in that flesh. But His living was in a humanity in resurrection.

When Nathanael came to Jesus, Jesus said something to him in resurrection: "Before Philip called you, while you were under the fig tree, I saw you" (John 1:48). He saw Nathanael under that tree far away because of His divinity with the divine ability, but that divine ability was in His humanity. Divinity is resurrection. Resurrection is a divine person, God. Only God is the resurrection that can stand against death, overcome death, enter into death, have a tour of death, and come out of death.

The One who created Adam came to be a man and lived a human life in resurrection. He denied His natural humanity. He never did anything out of Himself (John 5:19, 30). He did everything in Himself but not of Himself. We also should not do anything in our natural life but in Christ's resurrection life. Jesus was living and walking on this earth in His flesh, but He rejected this flesh. He rejected His natural life.

When Jesus was twelve years old, His parents took Him to Jerusalem to celebrate the Feast of the Passover. When they were returning from Jerusalem, they did not find Him, so they went back to search for Him. When they found Him in the temple, His mother said to Him, "Child, why have You treated us like this? Behold, Your father and I, being greatly distressed, have been seeking You." He responded, "Why is it that you were seeking Me? Did you not know that I must be in the things of My Father?" (Luke 2:48-49). In His humanity He was the son of His parents, but in His divinity He was the Son of God the Father. This shows that He rejected His natural life. He was living as a young boy in His divinity. In other words, He was not living by His natural man, born of Mary; He was living by His life in resurrection. His cherishing others to charm and attract them was not in His natural humanity, but in His humanity in resurrection.

Some people are charming, attractive, and cherishing in their natural humanity by birth. When such a person walks into a room, the atmosphere changes. A charming person must be very warm, not cold. Those who are charming in their natural humanity, however, are not real. Actually, they are performers, like actors in a theater. When you get close to a charming man, you will find out that he actually is not that charming. He was born with a mask. When the mask is taken away, he is different. To cherish people in our natural humanity is not genuine. This is why we must cherish people in the humanity of Jesus. The Lord's charming and cherishing are not natural but are by His resurrection life in humanity.

II. THE HUMANITY OF THE NEW MAN
OF THE BELIEVERS IN GOD'S NEW CREATION
IS ALSO IN RESURRECTION

The humanity of the new man of the believers in God's new creation is also in resurrection (Eph. 4:23-24). In the new creation, we are exactly the same as Jesus. We were reborn, regenerated, not with Adam's life but with Christ's life. Ephesians 2 says that we were once dead in offenses and sins, but God made us alive together with Christ and raised us up together with Him (vv. 1, 5-6). The crucified Christ was quickened, made alive, and we were made alive with Him. After this resurrection follows. We were made alive with Him and then we were resurrected with Him. Regeneration firstly makes us alive and then raises us up from the dead. Actually, regeneration itself is resurrection. Regeneration made us God's new creation (2 Cor. 5:17). This is the main stress in the New Testament.

Some deny that Christ resurrected with His humanity, but this teaching is wrong. He became the resurrected Christ with a resurrected humanity. Even while He was walking on this earth before He was resurrected, He was living in resurrection. Whatever He did was in His resurrected humanity, not the natural humanity. We can see this kind of living with the apostle Paul. He said, "I am crucified with Christ; and it is no longer I who live, but it is Christ who lives in me; and the life which I now live in the flesh I live in faith" (Gal. 2:20). Paul said that he no longer lived, but then he said, "I live." The "I" who now lives is a new "I" in resurrection. In other words, it is no longer I who live, Christ lives in me, yet I still live. Now I live a life that is not the natural life. My natural life has been crucified and resurrected. Now the life that I live is in resurrection.

Regeneration is resurrection, but do we live like a regenerated, resurrected, person? Do we live in resurrection or in our natural life? We have to admit that most of our daily living still remains in the natural life, not in resurrection. To be in resurrection means to be in Christ as the embodiment of the Triune God realized as the consummated Spirit. God, the Divine Trinity, the Father, the Son, and the Spirit, is resurrection.

God did not create Adam in resurrection but in the natural realm. God's placing Adam in front of the tree of life indicates that Adam needed another life. This life is Christ. The New Testament shows that Christ is the real tree of life (John 15:1; 14:6; Rev. 2:7). Eventually, in the new testament age, many of the descendants of Adam partook of the tree of life. This is the life of God, the life of Christ, the life of resurrection. Today we should live a life in this resurrection.

In Philippians 3:10 Paul said that he desired to know Christ, the power of His resurrection, and the fellowship of His sufferings, being conformed to His death. In order to experience Christ as the resurrection, we must always deny our self. Our self is a sinful self, but Christ's self was not sinful. Even though His self was not sinful, He still rejected Himself. He said, "The words that I say to you I do not speak from Myself," and, "The word which you hear is not Mine, but the Father's who sent Me" (John 14:10, 24). This shows that the Lord Jesus lived by another source in resurrection. This is very deep and very touching. Especially in these last few years, nearly every day I have been under a strong light. Under this light, I am checked within by the Lord: "Is this from yourself or from another person? Is this from your natural life or from the life of Christ?" This life is the Triune God Himself, who is resurrection.

When we contact people, we should not put on a mask. This is hypocrisy. Instead, we should be persons who are crucified in ourselves and resurrected in Christ. Then we will live in the same way that Jesus lived. We will be genuinely charming without any masks. Any kind of humility that comes from our natural life is false and ugly. It is performed with a mask. Both our pride and our humility should be crossed out. Then we do not live by our self. Instead, we live in our humanity by another life, by Christ who indwells us. He is living and real because He is the resurrection. We have such a One living in us.

We should not teach people to be humble, because this does not work. To teach people to be humble is to teach them to wear a mask. Paul's teaching is real. His teaching breaks our mask. In our teaching on character, we have shared that we need to be genuine, exact, and strict. But this is possible only for a resurrected person. In human history, there was only one person, Jesus the Nazarene, who was genuine, exact, and strict. He did not perform, but He lived in a spontaneous and genuine way. As members of the vital groups, we must be such persons. Then we will cherish people. When we contact people, they will be touched by us because we are living in resurrection. Then our humanity is not the original humanity but the crucified and resurrected humanity.

Before Jesus was crucified and resurrected, He lived a life in resurrection. Jesus was in resurrection before He was resurrected. He was a person living a human life in resurrection, not by Himself, but by another source, that is, His Father. Thus, He could say that when He spoke, that was the Father working within Him (John 14:10). He was one with the Father. If we live such a life today, a life in humanity by resurrection, everyone will realize that there is something different about us. We will be sweet, charming, and attractive, without deception or hypocrisy.

In order to be vital as members of the vital groups, we must be such persons. When we visit people, we must have the Lord's presence. His presence is the charming factor, and that presence comes from the cross plus resurrection. We must be a person on the cross and in resurrection. Then we will have the real presence of the Triune God with us, and that presence is resurrection.

How can we be vital? We may say that we have to pray much. This is right, but we need to see that the real prayer is by a person crucified in resurrection. If we are not a person crucified in resurrection, we cannot pray much. The genuine prayer means crucifixion plus resurrection. Crucifixion plus resurrection means everything to us Christians. If we are such persons, right away the Triune God is with us, and His presence goes with us wherever we go. When the divine presence is with us, people will not be able to explain or designate this, but they will sense that we are different, and they will be attracted to the Lord.

We can experience this only by being crucified and resurrected. This is stressed by Paul in Philippians 3:10. In order to know Christ, we have to know the power of His resurrection to be conformed to His death. His death should be a mold to which we are conformed. By experiencing Christ in this way, resurrection will be our portion, and we will have His presence. This presence is the Triune God as resurrection experienced by us in our being crucified and conformed to the death of Christ.

III. THE FIRST WAY TO CONTACT PEOPLE

The first way of the members of the vital group to contact people is by cherishing them. Because we live by our natural life, our visitation is fruitless.

IV. TO CHERISH PEOPLE

To cherish people is to make them happy, to comfort them, to make them feel that you are pleasant to them, easy to be contacted in everything and in every way. Our contact with people must be so genuine. Genuineness can be produced only by the cross plus resurrection. Only a crossed-out, resurrected person can be genuine in everything.

V. NOT BY OUR NATURAL MAN BUT BY OUR REGENERATED MAN

We should cherish people, not by our natural man, but by our regenerated man that has been conformed to the death of Christ. We have two men within us. Ephesians 4:22-24 reveals that we must put off the old man and put on the new man by being renewed in the spirit of our mind. The mingled spirit must invade, take over, occupy, and saturate our mind with divinity; then our mind becomes a renewed mind. Romans 12:2 says that we are to be transformed by the renewing of our mind. That renewing is to put off the old man and put on the new man. We must be a new man living not by our natural man but by our regenerated man with God Himself.

VI. THE MODEL OF JESUS IN CHERISHING PEOPLE IN HIS HUMANITY

A. In the Gospel of Matthew

1. Cherishing People by Shining over Them

As the King of the kingdom of the heavens in His humanity, Christ came to cherish people by shining over them as the great light and by preaching the kingdom of the heavens as the gospel by charging them to repent (4:12-17). We should be such a shining light by cherishing people in the humanity of Jesus.

2. Cherishing the Kingdom-seekers
by Blessing Them

As the human King of the kingdom of the heavens, Christ cherished the kingdom-seekers by blessing them with a ninefold blessing (5:1-12). Christ's mouth was full of blessing not cursing. When we visit people, our mouth must be filled up with the divine blessing. Our blessing people in this way is our cherishing them.

3. Moved with Compassion for the Crowd

When the disciples asked Him to dismiss the crowd to buy food for themselves, He, being moved with compassion for the crowd, told the disciples to give what they had to the people for them to eat that He might nourish the five thousand with five loaves and two fish, having a leftover of twelve baskets (14:14-21). The disciples are like us. When it became late in the day, they wanted the crowd to buy food for themselves, but the Lord was moved with compassion for them to cherish them which resulted in their being nourished.

4. Moved with Compassion for the Crowd Again

The Lord did the same thing in 15:32-38. This time He cherished and nourished four thousand.

5. Cherishing the Parents
by Laying His Hands on Their Children

When His disciples rejected people bringing their children to Him, He stopped their preventing and asked them to bring the children to Him, and He cherished the parents by laying His hands on their children (19:13-15). The disciples' preventing surely offended the parents. Quite often we are preventing people instead of cherishing people. The Lord stopped the disciples' preventing.

B. In the Gospel of Luke

1. Cherishing People with the Words of Grace
Proceeding out of His Mouth

Christ as the Man-Savior came to a synagogue in

Nazareth and read a portion from Isaiah that says, "The Spirit of the Lord is upon Me, because He has anointed Me to announce the gospel to the poor; He has sent Me to proclaim release to the captives, and recovery of sight to the blind, to send away in release those who are oppressed, to proclaim the acceptable year of the Lord, the year of jubilee," to cherish people with the words of grace proceeding out of His mouth (4:16-22). If we were the Lord, we might have read the law from Exodus 20 to the people instead of the jubilee of grace from Isaiah 61. To read the law to them would have condemned them. Instead, the Lord read a portion from Isaiah to them to cherish them with the words of grace proceeding out of His mouth.

2. Eating and Drinking with the Tax Collectors and Sinners

Christ as the Son of Man came to eat and drink with the tax collectors and sinners, even as their friend, to cherish them that they might be nourished by Him with His redemption and salvation (7:34). The Pharisees criticized the Lord for this, but His making friends with these sinful people was to lay the foundation so that He could nourish them with His redemption and salvation.

3. Cherishing Zaccheus

Christ as the Son of Man went to Jericho, passed by the tree from which Zaccheus was expecting to see Him, and looked up and said to him, "Zaccheus, hurry and come down, for today I must stay in your house," in order to cherish him that He might nourish him with His salvation (19:1-10).

C. In the Gospel of John

1. Cherishing Nathanael

When Christ as the God-Savior was recognized by Nathanael as the Son of God, He answered him that he would see heaven opened and the angels of God ascending and descending on Him as the Son of Man, like the heavenly ladder seen by Jacob in his dream, as a kind of cherishing to encourage

Nathanael to follow Him that he might participate in His nourishment with all the divine benefits as revealed in the entire Gospel of John (1:45-51).

Christ in His humanity is the standing ladder. The ark with the tabernacle, built of acacia wood overlaid with gold, is also a type of Christ. Acacia wood signifies Christ's humanity, and gold signifies Christ's divinity. This wood is the standing part; the gold is the overlaying part. To stand we need to be human in resurrection. Jesus became the ladder not by His divinity but by His humanity, not by Him as the Son of God but by Him as the Son of Man. He is the heavenly ladder, the uplifted stairway, to bring heaven to earth and to join earth to heaven for the building of the house of God.

2. Cherishing an Immoral Woman of Samaria

When Christ as the God-Savior wanted to save an immoral woman of Samaria, He had to travel from Judea to Galilee through Samaria and detoured from the main way of Samaria to the city of Sychar, and He waited at the well of Jacob, near Sychar, for His object to come that He might cherish her by asking her to give Him something to drink so that He might nourish her with the water of life, which is the flowing Triune God Himself (4:1-14). On His way to Galilee, Christ had to detour to a city in Samaria to cherish an immoral woman. He waited at the well of Jacob for her to come in order to cherish her so that she could be nourished with the living water of the Triune God.

3. Cherishing an Adulterous Woman

When none of the accusing Pharisees could condemn the adulterous woman, Christ as the God-Savior, in His humanity, said to her, "Neither do I condemn you," to cherish her that He, as the great I Am, might nourish her with the freedom from sin and enable her to "sin no more" (8:3-11, 24, 34-36). Christ is the divine, great "I Am," who can set people free from sin.

THE VITAL GROUPS

NOURISHING PEOPLE IN THE DIVINITY OF CHRIST

OUTLINE

I. The members of the vital groups have to learn how to nourish people to continue their cherishing of people.

II. To cherish people is to make them happy, pleasant, and comfortable; to nourish people is to feed them with the all-inclusive Christ in His full ministry in His three stages.

III. Both cherishing people and nourishing people should be by the divine and mystical life in resurrection, not by the natural life in the old creation.

IV. The model of Christ cherishing the churches and nourishing the churches in taking care of the churches—Rev. 1:12-13:

  A. He takes care of the churches as the lampstands in His humanity as "the Son of Man" to cherish them—v. 13a:

   1. By dressing the lamps of the lampstand—Exo. 30:7.

   2. By trimming the wicks of the lamps of the lampstand—Exo. 25:38.

  B. He, as the High Priest, takes care of the churches as the lampstands in His divinity with His divine love, signified by the golden girdle on His breasts, to nourish the churches—Rev. 1:13b:

   1. With His divine and mystical ministry by love in His three stages.

   2. That the churches may grow and mature in His divine life and become the overcomers in His sevenfold intensification.

In the previous message, we saw that we need to cherish people in the humanity of Jesus. To cherish people is to make them feel happy and comfortable. To nourish them is to feed them, to give them something to eat. In Ephesians 5 Paul speaks about Christ's care for the church by these two things: cherishing and nourishing (v. 29).

I. LEARNING HOW TO NOURISH PEOPLE

The members of the vital groups have to learn how to nourish people to continue their cherishing of people. Cherishing without nourishing is in vain. When a mother wants to feed a naughty child, she will first make him happy by cherishing him. But without nourishing him, her cherishing is meaningless. After cherishing the child, the mother nourishes him with food. This is the way that Christ as the Head takes care of His Body, the church. He nourishes us after cherishing us.

Revelation 1 shows us how Christ cares for the churches. Revelation is a book of signs. A sign is a symbol with spiritual significance. The first sign in Revelation shows us Christ in His humanity as the High Priest, and the last sign is the New Jerusalem. As the Son of Man, Christ as the High Priest is taking care of all the churches as lampstands (1:12-13). On the one hand, He is cherishing the churches in His humanity; on the other hand, He is nourishing the churches in His divinity. The members of the vital groups have to learn these two things. When we visit people, invite them to our home, or contact them before and after the meetings, we must be one with Christ to cherish and nourish them.

II. THE MEANING OF CHERISHING AND NOURISHING PEOPLE

To cherish people is to make them happy and to make them feel pleasant and comfortable. We must have a pleasant countenance when we contact people. We should be happy and rejoicing. We should not contact anyone with a cheerless countenance. We must give people the impression that we are genuinely happy and pleasant. Otherwise, we will not be able to cherish them, to make them happy.

Then we should go on to nourish them. We do not nourish people when we speak to them about marriage, courtship, politics, the world situation, or education. To nourish people is to feed them with the all-inclusive Christ in His full ministry in three stages. When we speak to people about Christ, we should not speak to them in an incomprehensible way in a kind of language which they do not understand. We have to find a way to present the all-inclusive Christ to everyone. If a person wants people to eat beef, he must find a way to cook it to make them desire to eat it. Similarly, we have to "cook" the all-inclusive Christ. There are many different ways to cook the same thing. I have been cooking Christ in this country for over thirty-three years with about three thousand messages.

In order to nourish people with Christ, we first have to seek Christ, experience Christ, gain Christ, enjoy Christ, and participate in Christ. In Philippians, especially in chapters two and three, Paul used different expressions and utterances to portray how he was seeking and pursuing Christ in order to gain Christ. He told us that we should do all things without murmurings and reasonings. The sisters who are seeking Christ should learn not to murmur, and the brothers should learn not to reason. If you murmur and reason, you will offend the indwelling Christ, who is the embodiment of the Triune God, because this God is working in you that you may work out your salvation (2:12-14). Our salvation is our gaining and experiencing Christ. To gain Christ is to work out our own daily organic salvation.

III. BY THE DIVINE AND MYSTICAL LIFE IN RESURRECTION

Both cherishing people and nourishing people should be by the divine and mystical life in resurrection, not by the natural life in the old creation. When something divine is operating in a human being, this human being becomes very mystical. When I was a young man, I worked for more than seven and a half years in a big corporation. Suddenly, I resigned from my job so that I could preach Christ with all of my time. They asked me how I could make a living. My

answer was that the Lord Jesus would provide for me. I
became mystical to my classmates and friends and also to
my relatives. They could not understand why I would give
up my job to serve the Lord with all of my time. I was a
mystery to them.

We should cherish people by the divine and mystical life
in resurrection. *In resurrection* means that there is nothing
natural in our care for people. Anything that is of our natural
life should not be used. Our life must be in resurrection. In
other words, our natural life must be crucified and resurrected to become a human life in resurrection. The young
people have to learn how to labor in the gospel on the college
campuses not by their natural life but by God within them as
their life. This is the divine life, and this divine life makes us
a mystery. Someone whom you contact may ask you where you
have graduated from and what kind of degree you have. You
may say that you have a degree from Harvard in biochemis-
try. They may ask, "What are you doing here?" When you say
that you are learning to preach Christ, they will not be able to
understand what kind of person you are. They would consider, "This person has graduated from a top university with
an excellent degree. The whole world needs him. He could get
an excellent job. Why would he come here to preach Christ?"
This makes you a mystical person. You have been educated
highly, but you are now doing a job which seemingly is not
that high but very mystical. You have become a divine,
mystical person in resurrection.

We must realize that the sevenfold intensified life-giving
Spirit only honors things in resurrection. If you do any work
which is not in resurrection, the life-giving Spirit will never
honor it. Thus, your labor will be in vain, with no result. Most
of the work in today's Christianity is not in resurrection.
Most Christians work in their natural life, not by the divine
and mystical life in resurrection. Anything that is natural
belongs to the old creation. Our contact with people should
not be in the old creation but in resurrection. It is only in this
way that we can cherish and nourish people with Christ, the
all-inclusive One.

IV. THE MODEL OF CHRIST CHERISHING
THE CHURCHES AND NOURISHING THE CHURCHES
IN TAKING CARE OF THE CHURCHES

Christ is the best model of cherishing and nourishing as seen in Revelation 1. In verses 12 and 13 John said, "I turned to see the voice that spoke with me; and when I turned, I saw seven golden lampstands, and in the midst of the lampstands One like the Son of Man, clothed with a garment reaching to the feet, and girded about at the breasts with a golden girdle." This shows that Christ is taking care of the lampstands by being the Son of Man with a long garment. This garment is the priestly robe (Exo. 28:33-35), which shows that Christ is our great High Priest.

He is also girded about at the breasts with a golden girdle. This girdle is a long piece of gold. The girdle and the gold are not two separate things. The girdle is the gold. The golden girdle is one piece of gold to become a belt. The Son of Man is in His humanity, and the golden girdle signifies His divinity. This golden girdle is on His breasts, and the breasts are a sign of love.

The priests in the Old Testament were girded at the loins for their ministry (Exo. 28:4). In Daniel 10:5 Christ also is girded at His loins, with fine gold. To be girded at the loins is to be strengthened for the work. Christ has finished His divine work in producing the churches. Now by His love He is caring for the churches which He has produced. This is why He is girded at the breasts. Today Christ is our High Priest taking care of His churches established by His labor. But now He takes care of the churches with the girdle not on His loins but on His breasts, signifying love. I hope we all could realize that in these days even among us, Christ is wearing a golden girdle on His breasts.

The golden girdle is a sign, signifying Christ's divinity becoming His energy. Christ's energy is totally His divinity. A piece of gold is now a girdle. The totality of Christ in His divinity has become a girdle. The golden girdle signifies Christ's divinity becoming His energy, and the breasts signify that this golden energy is exercised and motivated by His

love. His divine energy is exercised by and with His love to
nourish the churches.

A. Taking Care of the Churches in His Humanity

Christ takes care of the churches as the lampstands in His
humanity as "the Son of Man" to cherish them (Rev. 1:13a).
Christ as our High Priest takes care of the churches He has
established first in His humanity to cherish the churches, to
make the churches happy, pleasant, and comfortable.

1. By Dressing the Lamps

He does this by dressing the lamps of the lampstand.
The high priest in the Old Testament dressed the lamps of
the lampstands every morning (Exo. 30:7). To dress the lamps
is to make them proper.

2. By Trimming the Wicks

Christ cares for the lampstands by trimming the wicks of
the lamps of the lampstand, just as the priest did according to
the type in the Old Testament (Exo. 25:38). When the wick
was burned out it became charred and black, so the priest had
to come to cut off the black part of the wick. This is what it
means to snuff the wick so that the lamp may shine better.
The charred part of the wick, the snuff, signifies things that
are not according to God's purpose which need to be cut off,
such as our flesh, our natural man, our self, and our old
creation. All the lampstands are organic. They are living
lampstands. Since each church is a living lampstand, each
church has much feeling. A church with charred wicks will
not feel comfortable.

About eight years ago, there was no feeling of happiness or
pleasantness with the church in Anaheim. This was because
of the black, burned out, charred wicks. But one day Christ
as our High Priest came to dress the lamps of the lampstand,
the church in Anaheim, by trimming the wicks to cut off all
the black, charred wicks. This was a cherishing, to make the
church in Anaheim happy, pleasant, and comfortable. There is
no comparison between the way the church in Anaheim was
eight years ago and the way it is today. Eight years ago it

was full of burned, black wicks, with no shining. The saints felt unhappy, unpleasant, and uncomfortable. But one day the Lord Jesus as the High Priest in His humanity came to snuff all the negative things. Then we became happy, pleasant, and comfortable. This is Christ's taking care of the church in His humanity to dress the lamps of the church.

I thank the Lord that today in His recovery He is the High Priest in His humanity. Hebrews 4 says that we do not have a High Priest who cannot be touched with the feeling of our weaknesses, but One who has been tempted in all respects like us, yet without sin (v. 15). Our Christ is the same as we are. He has been tempted in everything like us, so He can easily be touched with the feeling of our weaknesses. This means that He always sympathizes with our weaknesses in His humanity. He is the High Priest in His humanity taking care of us by cherishing us all the time.

B. Taking Care of the Churches in His Divinity

Christ, as the High Priest, takes care of the churches as the lampstands in His divinity with His divine love, signified by the golden girdle on His breasts, to nourish the churches (Rev. 1:13b). Christ is not only human but also divine. He is the Son of Man wearing a golden girdle, signifying His divinity as His divine energy. His divinity as the divine energy nourishes the churches in many ways.

Revelation 2 and 3 reveal Christ's care for the lampstands. On the one hand, He trims the wicks of the church lamps, cutting away all the wrongdoings, shortages, failures, and defects mentioned in the seven epistles to the seven churches. Christ did the best trimming work in His humanity to cherish the churches. On the other hand, in each of these seven epistles, we see Christ's nourishing.

In the first epistle to the church at Ephesus, Christ says, "To him who overcomes, to him I will give to eat of the tree of life, which is in the Paradise of God" (2:7). We may say that this is a prophecy referring to the kingdom age, in which the overcomers will enjoy Christ as the tree of life in God's Paradise. But if we do not enjoy Christ as the tree of life in the church life today, surely we will not participate in the tree of life in the kingdom age. According to my experience, today the church in Anaheim is a paradise to me. In this paradise I eat much of Christ as the tree of life every day. If I do not eat Christ here today, I will not eat Him in the kingdom age. I have to eat here first.

In the second epistle to Smyrna, a persecuted and suffering church, Christ said that He would give the crown of life to those who overcome (v. 10). A crown signifies victory. If we are not a victor today, overcoming persecution and suffering, how can we be victors in the kingdom? Our victory today is out of Christ's being our life. If we do not have such an enjoyment today, how can we wear the crown of life in the coming age?

The third epistle was to the church in Pergamos. Pergamos was a church married to the world. The Lord will give the overcomers in Pergamos to eat of the hidden manna (v. 17). In the Old Testament, a portion of manna was preserved in a golden pot concealed in the ark (Exo. 16:32-34; Heb. 9:4). Today we must enjoy the hidden Christ in God's golden divine nature. Then we will enjoy Christ as the hidden manna in the coming age. Also, the Lord will give us a white stone and a new name, signifying that we have become a transformed person to be material for God's building.

The Lord promised the overcomers in the church in Thyatira that they would have the authority to rule, to reign as kings, over the nations (Rev. 2:26). First, we need to reign as kings today. According to Romans 5:17 we must receive the Lord's abounding grace to reign in life today. If we do not reign as kings today in Christ's life, how can we be kings in the coming age to rule over the nations?

In His fifth epistle, the Lord told the church in Sardis that they were dead and dying. He promised the overcomers that they would be clothed in white garments (Rev. 3:5). White garments signify the walk and living that are not stained with deadness. The way the overcomers walk in this age will be a prize to them in the coming age. We have to become living so that we can have the white garments.

The Lord told the church in Philadelphia to hold fast to what they already had (v. 11). Those who overcome to hold fast what they have in the Lord's recovery will be built into the New Jerusalem, the temple of God, as a pillar (v. 12). In the seventh epistle, the Lord counseled the church in Laodicea to buy gold, white garments, and eyesalve to be saved from their degradation in lukewarmness (v. 18). He promised to dine with the ones who would open the door to Him (v. 20). We can see that this is the nourishing of Christ in His divinity exercised by and with His love.

1. With His Divine and Mystical Ministry by Love in His Three Stages

He is also the High Priest with His divinity as the "energy belt" to nourish us with Himself as the all-inclusive Christ in His full ministry of three stages.

2. That the Churches May Grow and Mature in His Divine Life

His nourishing the churches in His divinity is so that the churches may grow and mature in His divine life and become the overcomers in His sevenfold intensification.

Our Christ today is our High Priest. In His humanity He is easily touched with the feeling of our weaknesses. He sympathizes with our weakness because He was tempted in all respects like us. He is cherishing us in His humanity. Meanwhile, He is nourishing us in His divinity with all the positive aspects of His person revealed in the seven epistles to the seven churches in Revelation 2 and 3. He is taking care of the churches in the recovery in both ways. In His humanity He is cherishing us to make us proper so that we may be happy, pleasant, and comfortable. In His divinity He is nourishing us so that we may grow and mature in the divine life to be His overcomers to accomplish His eternal economy.

THE VITAL GROUPS

NOURISHING PEOPLE
WITH THE UNSEARCHABLE RICHES
OF CHRIST IN HIS FULL MINISTRY
IN THE THREE STAGES

(1)

OUTLINE

I. The three stages of Christ:
   A. The stage of incarnation.
   B. The stage of inclusion.
   C. The stage of intensification.
II. The full ministry of Christ:
   A. All the works of Christ's accomplishments.
   B. From His incarnation to the consummation of the New Jerusalem.
III. The accomplishments of Christ in the stage of His incarnation:
   A. Bringing the infinite God into the finite man.
   B. Uniting and mingling the Triune God with the tripartite man.
   C. Expressing in His humanity the bountiful God in His rich attributes through His aromatic virtues:
      1. Expressing the bountiful God in His human living.
      2. Mainly expressing God in His rich attributes, that is, in the unsearchable riches of what God is.
      3. Through His aromatic virtues by which He attracted and captivated people:
         a. Not by living His human life in the flesh.
         b. But by living His divine life in resurrection.

D. Finishing His all-inclusive judicial redemption:
1. Terminating all things of the old creation.
2. Redeeming all the things created by God and fallen in sin—Heb. 2:9; Col. 1:20.
3. Creating (conceiving) the new man with His divine element—Eph. 2:15.
4. Releasing His divine life from the shell of His humanity—John 12:24.
5. Laying a foundation for His organic salvation and setting up the procedure to attain His ministry in the stage of His inclusion.

In the previous messages, we have seen how Christ cherishes us in His humanity and nourishes us in His divinity. Surely these are new terms in a new language. My burden is to minister something new, yet still ancient. The New Testament was written in a particular way. Each of the four Gospels has a particular way to minister Christ to us. The most particular and mysterious one is the Gospel of John.

We should not present Christ to others in an old or traditional way but in a new way according to the revelation of the rich Christ revealed in the New Testament. We may say to someone: "Christ is the very God who created the universe. One day He was born of a human virgin to be a man by the name of Jesus." This way of speaking is right and good. Although I appreciate it, I would still say that it is old. Because the United States is an old Christian nation, many people have already heard this kind of presentation of Christ. We have to learn to present Christ in a new way. We want to nourish people with the unsearchable riches of Christ in His full ministry in three stages.

When we go to visit people, we do not want to merely tell them something but to nourish them with Christ as their food. The first time I saw that the believers of Christ should learn how to eat Him was in 1958 in Taiwan. John 6:57 reveals that Jesus is edible: "He who eats Me, he also shall live because of Me." Of course, we live by what we eat. Actually, the Bible begins with the thought of God's desire for man to eat the tree of life. God created a perfect man, Adam, but God put this man in front of the tree of life. He did not put man in front of a book teaching him many things, including how to live a marriage life. God, after creating a perfect man, brought that man into a garden which included the tree of life. God warned this man not to eat the other tree, the tree of knowledge (Gen. 2:9, 16-17). Man must eat the right tree or he will be poisoned.

Man needs to eat only one thing—the tree of life. This tree signifies Christ. When Christ was incarnated, He said, "I am...the life" (John 14:6); He also said, "I am the vine" (John 15:5a). He is the life and He is the vine tree, so He is the tree of life. Christ is not only our Savior and Redeemer but also our life-tree. He is our food so that we can be nourished with Him. When we contact people, we should always endeavor to present some spiritual food to them, not to teach them with mere knowledge. Then they will be nourished. Ephesians 3:8 says that Christ's riches are unsearchable, or untraceable. The one new testament age reveals an unsearchably rich Christ in His full ministry in three stages.

I. THE THREE STAGES OF CHRIST

A. The Stage of Incarnation

First, Christ was incarnated to be a man. Then He lived on this earth for thirty-three and a half years. He died on the cross, and His crucifixion ended His stage of incarnation.

B. The Stage of Inclusion

His crucifixion ushered Him into another stage. After His death, He resurrected and entered into the stage of inclusion. In this stage Christ is the all-inclusive Spirit. He is now God, man, and also the all-inclusive, life-giving Spirit (1 Cor. 15:45b; 2 Cor. 3:17).

C. The Stage of Intensification

According to the flesh, Christ was the last Adam. Then as the last Adam, He became the life-giving Spirit. The book of Revelation shows that as the life-giving Spirit, He became the sevenfold intensified Spirit (Rev. 1:4; 3:1; 4:5; 5:6). We call the above three stages of Christ the three i's: incarnation, inclusion, and intensification.

II. THE FULL MINISTRY OF CHRIST

The full ministry of Christ includes all the works of Christ's accomplishments. Christ accomplishes so much by His ministry, His service, from His incarnation to the consummation of the New Jerusalem. The New Testament begins with Christ's incarnation and ends with the New Jerusalem. Matthew presents the birth of Christ, His incarnation, and Revelation presents the New Jerusalem, the holy city.

III. THE ACCOMPLISHMENTS OF CHRIST
IN THE STAGE OF HIS INCARNATION

The stage of Christ's incarnation was in the flesh, in His humanity, from His birth to His death.

A. Bringing the Infinite God into the Finite Man

The first thing Christ accomplished in His incarnation was to bring the infinite God into the finite man. When we contact an unbeliever, we can say, "I want to tell you that Christ has brought the infinite God into the finite man." This will stir up his interest and he will want to hear more. By ministering Christ with these attractive, new terms, we can gain people.

B. Uniting and Mingling the Triune God with the Tripartite Man

God is triune and man is tripartite. Christ in His incarnation united and mingled these two parties—the wonderful God, who is triune, and the excellent man, who is tripartite. Some people may have heard that God is triune, but not many know that man is of three parts. If we share Christ with them in this new terminology, they will be attracted and will want to hear more.

C. Expressing in His Humanity the Bountiful God in His Rich Attributes through His Aromatic Virtues

The utterance for this point is entirely new. Christ in His incarnation came to earth not only to bring the infinite God into the finite man and to unite and mingle the Triune God with the tripartite man, but also to express the bountiful God in His humanity, His human living. God is bountiful in His rich and many attributes. The attributes of God are what God is. He is love, light, holiness, and righteousness. We all admire humility. The real humble One is God. He was the infinite God, but He humbled Himself to become a finite man. Philippians 2:6-7 says that He existed in the form of God, but He took the form of a slave, becoming in the likeness of men. Verse 8 says, "And being found in fashion as a man,

He humbled Himself, becoming obedient even unto death, and that the death of a cross." He was in the form of God, but He humbled Himself to put on the form of man, becoming obedient to God, even unto the death of the cross. He became a servant, washing the feet of His disciples (John 13:1-11). God is the real One that is humble. Humility is one of the many attributes of God. God's attributes were expressed in Christ as a man to be Christ's virtues. Christ expressed the bountiful God in His human living, mainly expressing God in His rich attributes, that is, in the unsearchable riches of what God is. We have to study these things so that we can acquire these new points with these new terms.

When the attributes of God became the virtues of Christ in His humanity, these virtues were very aromatic and sweet. This is why so many people throughout the centuries have been captivated by Jesus and love Jesus. In my youth I was occupied with the world, but then I was captivated by the aromatic Christ. He is so sweet and good. Christ attracted and captivated people not by living His human life in the flesh but by living His divine life in resurrection. The incarnated Christ had two statuses. He was the Son of Man and the Son of God, having the human life and the divine life. Although He lived in the human life, He did not live by the human life. He lived His divine life in resurrection. His human life was always put aside. He said that He did not do anything out of Himself but that the Father was the source of all that He did (John 5:19, 30). He did not do anything in His natural life but He did everything in His divine life in resurrection. He always put His natural life on the cross, and through the cross He entered into resurrection. It should be the same with us today. A brother can talk to his wife in two ways. He can talk to her in his natural life, but this is wrong. He should talk to her in his natural, human life by another life, that is, the life of Christ, the divine life, the eternal life. We have to experience this. Then we can use this truth to nourish all those whom we contact.

D. Finishing His All-inclusive Judicial Redemption

In the stage of His incarnation, Christ brought the infinite

God into the finite man; He united and mingled the Triune God with the tripartite man; and He expressed in His humanity the bountiful God in His rich attributes through His aromatic virtues. Finally, He went to the cross to finish His all-inclusive judicial redemption. Most Christians say merely that Christ died on the cross for our sins so that we can be forgiven by God. This is true, but we need to go on to see Christ's death for our redemption in its deeper significance.

Christ died on the cross to terminate all things of the old creation. He also redeemed all the things created by God and fallen in sin (Heb. 2:9; Col. 1:20). On the cross He created (conceived) the new man with His divine element. Ephesians 2:15 says that Christ created in Himself both the Jews and Gentiles into one new man. Every conception requires a certain element. *In Himself* means in Himself as the divine element for this conceiving. In His redeeming death He also released His divine life from the shell of His humanity (John 12:24).

All of this laid a foundation for His organic salvation. His judicial, foundational redemption was accomplished through His death. Then His death ushered Him into resurrection for Him to exercise His organic salvation. Thus, His judicial redemption is a foundation of His organic salvation. Furthermore, His judicial redemption is not only a foundation but also a procedure to attain His ministry in the stage of His inclusion. We should endeavor to learn all the things presented in this message and in the following two messages concerning the unsearchably rich Christ in His full ministry in three stages.

THE VITAL GROUPS

NOURISHING PEOPLE
WITH THE UNSEARCHABLE RICHES
OF CHRIST IN HIS FULL MINISTRY
IN THE THREE STAGES

(2)

OUTLINE

IV. The accomplishments of Christ in the stage of His inclusion from His resurrection to the degradation of the church:

A. To be begotten as God's firstborn Son:

1. From eternity past without beginning, Christ was God's only begotten Son:

    a. Possessing only divinity, without humanity.

    b. Not having passed through death into resurrection.

2. In incarnation the only begotten Son of God became flesh to be a God-man, a man possessing both the divine nature and the human nature.

3. Through death and resurrection Christ in the flesh as the seed of David was designated to be the firstborn Son of God:

    a. In death His humanity was crucified.

    b. In resurrection His crucified humanity was made alive by the Spirit of His divinity and was uplifted into the sonship of the only begotten Son of God.

    c. Thus, He was begotten by God in His resurrection to be the firstborn Son of God.

B. To become the life-giving Spirit:

1. First Corinthians 15:45b says, "The last Adam [Christ in the flesh] became a life-giving Spirit."

2. This life-giving Spirit "was not yet" before the resurrection of Christ—the glorification of Christ—John 7:39.

3. Christ, the Son of God as the second of the Divine Trinity, after completing His ministry on the earth, became (was transfigured into) the life-giving Spirit in His resurrection:

   a. This life-giving Spirit is signified by the water that flowed out of the pierced side of Jesus on the cross—John 19:34.

   b. To release the divine life that was confined in the shell of Christ's humanity and to dispense it into His believers, making them the many members which constitute His Body—John 12:24.

4. This life-giving Spirit who is the pneumatic Christ is also called:

   a. The Spirit of life—Rom. 8:2.

   b. The Spirit of Jesus—Acts 16:7.

   c. The Spirit of Christ—Rom. 8:9.

   d. The Spirit of Jesus Christ—Phil. 1:19.

   e. The Lord Spirit—2 Cor. 3:18.

C. To regenerate the believers for His Body—1 Pet. 1:3:

1. The pneumatic Christ became the life-giving Spirit for the regenerating of the believers, making them the many sons of God born of God with Him in the one universally big delivery:

   a. For the composition of the house of God, even the household of God.

   b. For the constitution of the Body of Christ to be His fullness, His expression and expansion, to consummate the eternal expression and expansion of the processed and consummated Triune God:

    1) All the believers of Christ in this one Spirit have been baptized into the one Body of Christ—1 Cor. 12:13a.

    2) All the believers who are baptized in this one Spirit are given to drink this Spirit—1 Cor. 12:13b.

2. The Christ in resurrection giving Himself as the all-inclusive life-giving Spirit without measure through His speaking of the words of God—John 3:34.

3. All the believers in Christ are built up into a dwelling place of God in their spirit indwelt by Him as the Spirit—Eph. 2:22:

  a. Through dispositional sanctification—Rom. 15:16.

  b. Through renewing—Titus 3:5.

  c. Through transformation—2 Cor. 3:18.

  d. Through conformation—Rom. 8:29.

In the previous message we saw the accomplishments of Christ in the stage of His incarnation. Now we want to see His accomplishments in the stage of His inclusion from His resurrection to the degradation of the church. We need to be constituted with all the items of this revelation so that we can nourish people with the unsearchable riches of Christ in His full ministry in the three stages.

IV. THE ACCOMPLISHMENTS OF CHRIST IN THE STAGE OF HIS INCLUSION FROM HIS RESURRECTION TO THE DEGRADATION OF THE CHURCH

The degradation of the church began at the end of the early apostles' ministry. In Paul's second Epistle to Timothy we can see this degradation. We need to see the three major things which Christ accomplished in the stage of His inclusion from His resurrection to the degradation of the church. In Christ's resurrection He was begotten as God's firstborn Son, He became the life-giving Spirit, and He regenerated the believers for His Body.

An excellent illustration of Christ's death and resurrection was given by the Lord when He likened Himself to a grain of wheat falling into the earth to die and to bear much fruit in resurrection. After the grain of wheat is sown into the earth, on the one hand it is dying, but on the other hand it is rising up. The shell is dying, but the life element within the grain is growing. Eventually, a new sprout comes out from the death and resurrection of the grain. According to 1 Peter 3:18, Christ's resurrection was going on while He was dying on the cross. He was "on the one hand being put to death in the flesh, but on the other, made alive in the Spirit." According to His flesh He was crucified for our sins, but according to the Spirit He was very active. Resurrection was not a sudden event. Actually, while Christ was dying in the flesh on the cross, He was active, moving, and energized with life to rise up.

A. To Be Begotten as God's Firstborn Son

1. God's Only Begotten Son

From eternity past without beginning, Christ was God's only begotten Son, possessing only divinity, without humanity.

At that time He had not passed through death into resurrection.

2. Becoming Flesh to Be a God-man

In incarnation the only begotten Son of God became flesh to be a God-man, a man possessing both the divine nature and the human nature.

3. Designated to Be the Firstborn Son of God

Through death and resurrection, Christ in the flesh as the seed of David was designated to be the firstborn Son of God. In death His humanity was crucified. In resurrection His crucified humanity was made alive by the Spirit of His divinity and was uplifted into the sonship of the only begotten Son of God. Thus, He was begotten by God in His resurrection to be the firstborn Son of God.

B. To Become the Life-giving Spirit

1. The Last Adam (Christ in the Flesh) Became a Life-giving Spirit

First Corinthians 15:45b says, "The last Adam [Christ in the flesh] became a life-giving Spirit." The last Adam was the last man. Christ's crucifixion was the end of man. In His resurrection Christ, the last Adam, became the life-giving Spirit for dispensing life.

2. The Life-giving Spirit Being "Not Yet" before the Resurrection of Christ

According to John 7:39, prior to the glorification of Christ, the resurrection of Christ, "the Spirit was not yet." This means that the life-giving Spirit "was not yet" before the resurrection of Christ—the glorification of Christ. Before Christ was resurrected, the Spirit of God was not the life-giving Spirit.

3. Christ Being Transfigured into the Life-giving Spirit

Christ, the Son of God as the second of the Divine Trinity, after completing His ministry on the earth, became (was transfigured into) the life-giving Spirit in His resurrection. This life-giving Spirit is signified by the water that flowed out of the pierced side of Jesus on the cross (John 19:34). Through His death and resurrection, Christ released the divine life that was confined in the shell of His humanity and dispensed it into His believers, making them the many members which constitute His Body (John 12:24).

4. The Life-giving Spirit Being the Pneumatic Christ

This life-giving Spirit who is the pneumatic Christ is also called the Spirit of life (Rom. 8:2), the Spirit of Jesus (Acts 16:7), the Spirit of Christ (Rom. 8:9), the Spirit of Jesus Christ (Phil. 1:19), and the Lord Spirit (2 Cor. 3:18). *The Lord Spirit* may be considered a compound title like *the Father God* and *the Lord Christ*.

C. To Regenerate the Believers for His Body

First Peter 1:3 reveals that Christ regenerated all of us who believe in Him in His resurrection. With God there is no time element. According to our human perspective, we were regenerated at a certain time, but in God's view all of His many sons were regenerated through the resurrection of Christ. In Revelation nearly all the predicates are in the past tense. In the eyes of God the New Jerusalem has been completed already. We say that we are consummating the New Jerusalem, and this is correct according to our view in time. But according to God, He has already consummated the New Jerusalem. Revelation 13:8 says that the Lamb was slain from the foundation of the world. In the eternal view of God, from the time the created things came into being, Christ was crucified.

1. The Many Sons of God Born with Christ as the Firstborn Son in One Universally Big Delivery

The purpose of Christ's being begotten to be the firstborn Son of God and becoming the life-giving Spirit was for the regenerating of the believers, making them the many sons of God born of God with Him in the one universally big delivery. Christ's resurrection was a big delivery of Himself as the firstborn Son and the believers as His many brothers, His millions of "twins." This was for the composition of the house of God, even the household of God, and the constitution of the Body of Christ to be His fullness, His expression and expansion, to consummate the eternal expression and expansion of the processed and consummated Triune God. All the believers of Christ in this one Spirit have been baptized into the one Body of Christ (1 Cor. 12:13a). Furthermore, all the believers who are baptized in this one Spirit are given to drink this one Spirit (1 Cor. 12:13b). Through baptism we were immersed in the Spirit, and by drinking the Spirit gets into us. The best Christians are the ones who are in the Spirit and have the Spirit in them to make them completely one with the Spirit.

2. Giving the Spirit without Measure

The Christ in resurrection gave Himself as the all-inclusive life-giving Spirit without measure through His speaking of the words of God (John 3:34). The more we receive the Lord's words, the more we are filled with the immeasurable Spirit.

3. Being Built Up into a Dwelling Place of God in Spirit

All the believers in Christ are built up into a dwelling place of God in their spirit indwelt by Him as the Spirit (Eph. 2:22) through dispositional sanctification (Rom. 15:16), renewing (Titus 3:5), transformation (2 Cor. 3:18), and conformation (Rom. 8:29).

In order to get into the details of the outlines we have released on Christ in His three stages, I would like to recommend the practice of the saints in Taipei. They come together in small groups to pray-read the outline. After pray-reading they study it. Then they learn to recite the entire outline, word by word. Then they prophesy. We may feel that we cannot do this, but if there is a will, there is a way. This practice of pray-reading, studying, reciting, and prophesying has become the best way for the saints in Taipei to digest all these new outlines. After they practice this, they are fully nourished, and they can go to nourish others.

The content of one outline concerning Christ in one of His stages is like ten meals. We should nourish people with a meal. Each member of the vital groups should present a meal to people for their nourishment. It is hard to see a group among us today which is really vital. Our groups are not vital because we are not nourished. If we want to enter into the intrinsic significance of the Bible, we need to digest these outlines we have released to enable us to nourish others with the unsearchable riches of Christ in His full ministry in three stages.

THE VITAL GROUPS

NOURISHING PEOPLE
WITH THE UNSEARCHABLE RICHES
OF CHRIST IN HIS FULL MINISTRY
IN THE THREE STAGES

(3)

OUTLINE

V. The accomplishments of Christ in the stage of His intensification from the degradation of the church to the consummation of the New Jerusalem:
  A. To intensify His organic salvation:
    1. For His ministry in the stage of His inclusion, Christ became the life-giving Spirit, the pneumatic Christ, to carry out His organic salvation for the producing of the church and the building up of His Body to consummate the New Jerusalem.
    2. On the way of Christ's ministry in the stage of His inclusion, the church became degraded to frustrate the accomplishment of God's eternal economy.
    3. Hence, Christ as the one life-giving Spirit became the seven Spirits of God—Rev. 1:4; 4:5; 5:6; 3:1:
      a. Not seven individual Spirits.
      b. But the one Spirit who is intensified sevenfold.
      c. To intensify the organic salvation of Christ sevenfold for the building up of the Body of Christ to consummate God's eternal goal— the New Jerusalem.

B. To produce the overcomers:
   1. Through the degradation of the church nearly all the believers in Christ became defeated in their old man by Satan, sin, the world, and their flesh.
   2. In His seven epistles to the degraded churches, Christ calls the defeated believers to be His overcomers by Himself as the sevenfold intensified Spirit for their experience of His organic salvation in His sevenfold intensification.

C. To consummate the New Jerusalem:
   1. According to the entire revelation of the New Testament, the unique goal of the Christian work should be the New Jerusalem, which is the ultimate goal of God's eternal economy.
   2. The degradation of the church is mainly due to the fact that nearly all the Christian workers are distracted to take many things other than the New Jerusalem as their goal.
   3. Hence, under the degradation of the church, to be an overcomer answering the Lord's call needs us to overcome not only the negative things but even more the positive things which replace the New Jerusalem as the goal.
   4. An overcomer's goal should be uniquely and ultimately the goal of God's eternal economy, that is, the New Jerusalem.

V. THE ACCOMPLISHMENTS OF CHRIST
IN THE STAGE OF HIS INTENSIFICATION

In this message we want to see the accomplishments of Christ in the stage of His intensification from the degradation of the church to the consummation of the New Jerusalem. Recently we have seen that John 4:14b shows us that the goal of God's eternal economy is the New Jerusalem: "The water that I will give him will become in him a fountain of water springing up into eternal life." The Father is the fountain, the source, emerging in the Son as the spring, who flows out as the Spirit, the river, into eternal life. The phrase *into eternal life* means into the totality of the eternal life. Each human being is a totality of the human life. The totality, the aggregate, of the eternal life is the New Jerusalem. Our God is the flowing God, flowing to impart and dispense Himself as life into all His lovers. Eventually, this eternal life will have an aggregate, a totality, a consummation. That will be the New Jerusalem. The New Jerusalem is the totality of the eternal life in the entire Bible.

The apostle Paul said that we are God's farm to grow Christ and God's building (1 Cor. 3:9). As we grow in the divine life, we are transformed into precious material for God's building: gold, silver, and precious stones (v. 12). The New Jerusalem is constituted with transformed precious material: gold as the base, pearls as the gates, and precious stones for the city's wall. If we build up the church with ourselves, with the world, or with earthly things, we are building with wood, grass, and stubble, which are fit only to be burned (vv. 12b-13). But if we build the church with the Triune God—the Father as the gold, the Son as the pearl or silver, and the Spirit as the precious stone—our building work will be a part of the New Jerusalem. In other words, our work will go into eternal life. The New Jerusalem as the totality of the eternal life is God's goal. The chorus of *Hymns,* #976, a hymn concerning the New Jerusalem, says, "Lo, the holy city, / Full of God's bright glory! / It is God's complete expression / In humanity." Christ has become the sevenfold intensified Spirit to intensify His organic salvation and to produce the overcomers for the consummating of the New Jerusalem.

A. To Intensify His Organic Salvation

1. Christ Becoming the Life-giving Spirit, the Pneumatic Christ, in the Stage of His Inclusion

For His ministry in the stage of His inclusion, Christ became the life-giving Spirit, the pneumatic Christ, to carry out His organic salvation for the producing of the church and the building up of His Body to consummate the New Jerusalem.

2. The Church Becoming Degraded

On the way of Christ's ministry in the stage of His inclusion, the church became degraded to frustrate the accomplishment of God's eternal economy.

3. Christ as the One Life-giving Spirit Becoming the Seven Spirits of God

Hence, Christ as the one life-giving Spirit became the seven Spirits of God (Rev. 1:4; 4:5; 5:6; 3:1). These are not seven individual Spirits, but the one Spirit who is intensified sevenfold. This is to intensify the organic salvation of Christ sevenfold for the building up of the Body of Christ to consummate God's eternal goal—the New Jerusalem.

B. To Produce the Overcomers

1. Nearly All the Believers in Christ Becoming Defeated

Through the degradation of the church nearly all the believers in Christ became defeated in their old man by Satan, sin, the world, and their flesh.

2. Christ Calling the Defeated Believers to Be His Overcomers

In His seven epistles to the degraded churches, Christ calls the defeated believers to be His overcomers by Himself as the sevenfold intensified Spirit for their experience of His organic salvation in His sevenfold intensification.

C. To Consummate the New Jerusalem

1. The Unique Goal of the Christian Work

According to the entire revelation of the New Testament, the unique goal of the Christian work should be the New Jerusalem, which is the ultimate goal of God's eternal economy.

2. The Main Cause of the Church's Degradation

The degradation of the church is mainly due to the fact that nearly all the Christian workers are distracted to take many things other than the New Jerusalem as their goal.

3. Overcoming Everything Which Replaces the New Jerusalem as Our Goal

Hence, under the degradation of the church, to be an overcomer answering the Lord's call needs us to overcome not only the negative things but even more the positive things which replace the New Jerusalem as the goal.

4. An Overcomer's Goal

An overcomer's goal should be uniquely and ultimately the goal of God's eternal economy, that is, the New Jerusalem.

I want to encourage us once again to get the points of these outlines into us by following the pattern of the saints in Taiwan. They pray-read the outlines, study them, recite the points of the outlines, and then they speak these points to one another, that is, they prophesy. The churches in Taiwan have been revived by taking this way. If we take this way, I believe that the churches in Southern California will have a big revival.

THE VITAL GROUPS

MESSAGE FIFTEEN

HOW TO CONTACT PEOPLE

(1)

OUTLINE

  I. You should be one who is in the intimate and thorough fellowship with the Lord, without anything between the Lord and you.
 II. Having a thorough confession all the time of failures, defects, wrongdoings, practices of the flesh and of your natural man, offenses to God and men, and sins.
III. Praying thoroughly for your visiting of people and for those whom you visit and contact.
 IV. You must be so familiar with all the outlines of the recent messages concerning the person of Christ and His accomplishments in the three stages of His full ministry that you can memorize them and use them spontaneously in your visiting and contacting of people.

A TESTIMONY

The church life here has been very sweet. Up until now, we have been in localities where the church was small or had some difficult situations. This is the first time we feel like we ourselves are being (1) shepherded by the saints. (2) The saints here are genuinely pursuing Christ and building up the church according to the New Testament ministry. It is refreshing. It has also been exposing. I realize I have gotten somewhat old and cold. But I am getting warmed up again!

(3) Many of the saints are actively shepherding new ones at various stages. Also (4) at least half the

saints still go out door-knocking each week. (5) They have been practicing this for the last ten years! (6) New ones (mostly Caucasians) steadily come into the church life through door-knocking, and (7) contacting of neighbors, co-workers, and relatives. (8) In the meetings there has never been a gap in between the testimonies. It is hard to testify because there are so many who want to testify. (9) My own appetite has been stimulated by (10) the saints' intense and serious appetite for the ministry.

The Lord has shown us in this series of messages that we need to contact people by cherishing and nourishing them (Eph. 5:29). In the early part of this century, R. A. Torrey published a book entitled *How to Bring Men to Christ*. The Lord has taken us on to see that we need to cherish people in the humanity of Jesus and nourish them in the divinity of Christ. We cherish them with the goal of nourishing them with the unsearchable riches of Christ in His full ministry in three stages. In this message we want to continue our fellowship concerning how to contact people.

In 1984 I realized that the recovery, both in Taiwan and in America, had become dormant. Actually, we had become somewhat like Laodicea. They said they were rich, but they were poor in gold (Rev. 3:17-18). Gold is God Himself. The church in Laodicea was proud of being rich in the vain knowledge of doctrine, but they were poor in the reality of God Himself. The Lord prayed that the Father would sanctify us with His word because His word is truth, reality (John 17:17). Reality is the Triune God. Since the Triune God is contained in His word, His word is reality, and we are sanctified in the reality of this word.

The Brethren became like Laodicea because they were proud of their knowledge of many doctrines. Eventually, they were divided by their doctrinal teachings. They were raised up by the Lord at the beginning of the nineteenth century, but within a short period of time they became divided into about one thousand groups. Although they were rich in doctrine, their doctrine was not truth because it lacked the divine element. The divine element, the reality of God, is the gold. The Lord counseled the Laodiceans to buy gold for them to be rich. He also charged them to buy eyesalve to anoint their eyes that they might see. This means that despite their doctrinal knowledge, they did not have the true spiritual sight. They had no light, life, or reality. We must be warned by the Lord's word to Laodicea. We may be rich in the knowledge of the high peak of the divine revelation, but we should not think that we have the reality. The mere doctrine means nothing. My burden is to help us become vital and have the vitality to contact and gain people.

I. BEING A PERSON IN THE INTIMATE
AND THOROUGH FELLOWSHIP WITH THE LORD

In order to be vital, we should be ones who are in the intimate and thorough fellowship with the Lord, without anything between the Lord and us. If we are not such persons, we are not qualified to contact people for God's economy. Many in Christianity promote soul-winning. They may gain people, but most of the ones they gain are dying spiritually. We do not want to bring dead and dying people into the recovery. We must have the vitality to vitalize those whom we contact. The vitality is hidden in our intimate, thorough fellowship with the Lord, with nothing between us and the Lord. This makes us absolutely one with the Lord.

II. HAVING A THOROUGH CONFESSION

We must have a thorough confession all the time of our failures, defects, wrongdoings, practices of the flesh and of our natural man, our offenses toward God and men, and our sins. We want to remain in and be conformed to Christ's death (Phil. 3:10). We must confess that we have not been fully conformed to His death, especially in the way that we speak to our spouse. First John 1 says that if we say we do not have sin, we are lying (vv. 8, 10). If we say we have no sin, this means we are blind. We are full of sins, so we must make a thorough confession of our sins. Because our hands become dirty throughout the day, we have to wash them many times. In the same way, we must confess our sins to the Lord throughout the day to receive the continual cleansing of His blood.

III. PRAYING THOROUGHLY
FOR THOSE WHOM WE VISIT

We should pray thoroughly for our visiting of people and for those whom we visit and contact. We should not contact someone without praying for him. We should pray adequately and desperately for the people whom we contact. In the past I encouraged the saints to visit people by knocking on their doors once a week for about three hours. Those who go out should be able to stand on the thorough prayer they have had throughout the week. We should pray desperately that the Lord would make us fruitful. If each of us cannot gain one person for the Lord within a year, this is a shame. The Lord charged us to go and bear much fruit for the Father to be glorified (John 15:8, 16). We must keep the Lord's word to bear fruit, but we have not done this absolutely.

IV. BECOMING FAMILIAR WITH ALL THE OUTLINES OF THE RECENT MESSAGES CONCERNING THE PERSON OF CHRIST AND HIS ACCOMPLISHMENTS

We must be so familiar with all the outlines of the recent messages concerning the person of Christ and His accomplishments in the three stages of His full ministry. We can memorize them and use them spontaneously in our visiting and contacting of people. The churches in Taiwan have entered into the way of pray-reading, studying, reciting, and prophesying all the items of the outlines. If we practice this, we will be saturated and soaked with all these points, and we will have much of the truth to speak to others. If we take this way, we can become very useful in going out to speak to people. What we speak concerning the person of Christ according to the new light we have received will be very attractive to people, because they have never heard such things.

I have spent over ten years to help the churches enter into a vital situation. Recently, I received a testimony from someone which shows that at least one church has become vital. The contents of this testimony are printed below, and we have numbered the crucial points in it.

A TESTIMONY

The church life here has been very sweet. Up until now, we have been in localities where the church was small or had some difficult situations. This is the first time we feel like we ourselves are being (1) shepherded by the saints. (2) The saints here are genuinely pursuing Christ and building up the church according to the New Testament ministry. It is refreshing. It has also been exposing.

I realize I have gotten somewhat old and cold. But I am getting warmed up again!

(3) Many of the saints are actively shepherding new ones at various stages. Also (4) at least half the saints still go out door-knocking each week. (5) They have been practicing this for the last ten years! (6) New ones (mostly Caucasians) steadily come into the church life through door-knocking, and (7) contacting of neighbors, co-workers, and relatives. (8) In the meetings there has never been a gap in between the testimonies. It is hard to testify because there are so many who want to testify. (9) My own appetite has been stimulated by (10) the saints' intense and serious appetite for the ministry.

The person who wrote the above testimony said that he was shepherded by the saints, not by the elders or co-workers. This means that they practice the shepherding which the ministry teaches. We need to pay attention to the phrase *by the saints* in the above testimony.

The saints in this locality are pursuing Christ according to the New Testament ministry, not according to different teachings. Revelation 2 speaks of the teaching of Balaam (v. 14), the teaching of the Nicolaitans (v. 15), the teaching by Jezebel (v. 20), and the teaching of the deep things of Satan (v. 24). In today's Christianity, there are many different teachings, but we should have only one teaching, the New Testament teaching, which is called the apostles' teaching (Acts 2:42). The unique teaching in the New Testament is the teaching of the apostles concerning God's eternal economy to produce the church for the Body that consummates the New Jerusalem. When we pursue Christ and build up the church according to the apostles' teaching, the New Testament ministry, we will be under the Lord's blessing. We may say that it is difficult to gain Caucasians, but in the place mentioned above, at least half of the saints have faithfully practiced door-knocking for the past ten years, and the new ones they have gained have been mostly Caucasians. The contents of the above testimony are according to what I have been teaching for the past ten years. This testimony confirms that the God-ordained way to practice and build up the church life according to the New Testament ministry really works.

THE VITAL GROUPS

HOW TO CONTACT PEOPLE

(2)

We have seen that in all of our contact with people, we must cherish them with the goal of nourishing them with the unsearchable riches of Christ. We ourselves must be constituted with the riches of Christ revealed in the Bible, if we are going to dispense these riches into others.

The Bible was first written, then translated, and finally interpreted and explained. According to our old way, many of us have been listening to messages interpreting the Bible for years, but when we go to contact people, we still do not know what to say. This is why I have shared that we need to follow the pattern of the saints in Taiwan to practice PSRP—pray-reading, studying, reciting, and prophesying. All of this requires time. Pray-reading cannot be done lightly. Then we need to study the truths word by word, term by term, and phrase by phrase. For instance, John 1:1 says, "In the beginning was the Word, and the Word was with God, and the Word was God." Then verse 14 says that the Word became flesh and tabernacled among us, full of grace and reality. Many read these verses without understanding them. This is why we need the word to be interpreted to us.

Acts 8 gives us a very good example of this. The Ethiopian eunuch whom Philip contacted was reading from Isaiah, and Philip asked him, "Do you really know the things that you are reading?" The eunuch responded, "How could I unless someone guides me?" (vv. 30-31). Philip interpreted the word to this eunuch, and he believed in the Lord and was baptized (vv. 35-38). Some people have said that all we need is the "pure Word," but how can we understand it? Acts 8 shows that we need the Word interpreted to us.

Our study equips us to interpret the Word to others. By my study of the Word throughout the years, I saw that grace is God gained and enjoyed by us and reality is God realized by us. We have to gain Him, receive Him, and enjoy Him as grace. Then we have to realize Him as the reality. Although points like this have been made clear in our Life-study of the Bible, we may not pay attention to them to study them. In order to be constituted with the truth, we need to pray-read and then study. Pray-reading verses such as John 1:1 and 14 lays a good foundation. Then we can study the crucial points of these verses with the help of the life-studies. With this help we can find out what grace and reality are. We have to study the truths word by word, term by term, and phrase by phrase. Spontaneously, we will be able to recite what we have pray-read and studied. In addition to our personal study, we also need to study with others. This kind of study cannot be carried out in big meetings. It can be carried out mutually in vital group meetings of six to not more than ten saints.

We have inherited much from the foregoing interpretations of the Word and have had a life-study of the entire Bible. Then the Lord has taken us further to have a crystallization-study. In this study I have to spend time not merely to present messages as I did with the life-study, but to present outlines. We have to pray-read, study, recite, and prophesy with the points of these outlines. If we are equipped to recite the outlines, we will spontaneously know how to prophesy. The second point of outline one of the recent Thanksgiving conference says, "His [Christ's] humanity through His incarnation became a shell to conceal the glory of His divinity." In the beginning was the Word, who is God, this Word became flesh, and this flesh was a shell to conceal the glory of Christ's divinity. This is why the first banner of the conference says, "The glory of Christ's divinity was concealed in Him as in a grain of wheat." The shell of the grain of wheat conceals the grain's life and riches. If we prophesy with points like these, those whom we contact will want to hear what we say. This new way of pray-reading, studying, reciting, and prophesying—PSRP—has been passed on to many places. What I am speaking here is a kind of instruction to all the churches. My new way is PSRP. This is the way for us to cook and to eat the riches which have been released in these recent years.

Part of our upcoming winter training will be a crystallization-study of the Lord's organic salvation in Romans. Romans 5:10 says, "For if we, being enemies, were reconciled to God through the death of His Son, much more we will be saved in His life, having been reconciled." We should pray-read this verse and then study it. The subject *we* refers to the believers. At one time we were God's enemies, but we were reconciled to God by the death of His Son. The death of God's Son was for our judicial redemption. The salvation in Christ's life is for our organic salvation. We have to study these points and then recite them. Then we will be equipped to prophesy.

We should prophesy with what we can recite; what we can recite is what we have studied; and what we have studied is what we have pray-read. If we do not pray-read, study, or recite, we cannot prophesy. I have encouraged people to prophesy in the Lord's Day meeting, but they still claim that they do not know what to say. Now we have a new way. If we pray-read, study, and recite the points of the outlines released in our crystallization-study of the Word, we will surely prophesy. Who cannot prophesy? Those who do not pray-read the outline, who do not study the outline, and who do not recite the outline. If we practice PSR (pray-reading, studying, and reciting) each day, from Monday through Saturday, we will surely prophesy in the Lord's Day meeting of the church.

Before giving this message, I studied Philip's encounter with the Ethiopian eunuch in Acts 8. Verses 32 through 35 say, "Now the passage of Scripture which he [the eunuch] was reading was this: 'As a sheep He was led to slaughter; and as a lamb before its shearer is dumb, so He does not open His mouth. In His humiliation His judgment was taken away. Who shall declare His generation? For His life is taken away from the earth.' And the eunuch answered Philip and said, I beseech you, Concerning whom does the prophet say this? Concerning himself or concerning someone else? And Philip opened his mouth, and beginning from this Scripture he announced Jesus as the gospel to him." This was Philip's preaching of the gospel.

This account in Acts 8 shows that the practice of PSRP is not our new way. It was in the Bible already, in Acts 8. The way Philip answered the eunuch and preached Christ to him as the gospel surely indicates that Philip had studied that portion of Isaiah 53, which the eunuch quoted to him, and that he had remembered that portion so that he could preach Christ as the gospel as a kind of prophesying. If he were not familiar with that portion of the holy Word, how could he have preached Christ as the gospel according to that portion? His preaching was a real prophesying of the holy Word with which he had become familiar.

If anyone comes to the Lord's Day morning meeting without being prepared to prophesy, this indicates he was lazy for the whole week. Throughout the week, he did not pray-read, study, or recite. If he had practiced this, he would be able to prophesy on the Lord's Day. After reading the fellowship in this message, we may feel that the standard in the church is too high. In a sense, this is true because we are in the Lord's recovery. We do not want to remain in degraded Christianity. Those in Catholicism are required only to attend mass. They do not have to function. Those in Protestantism mostly listen to sermons. They are not required to speak for the Lord in their meetings. The Lord's recovery is different.

All of the members of Christ's Body should be functioning members who speak for the Lord. This is why we need to practice PSRP. We have to pray-read, study, and recite the points we have studied. Then spontaneously our pray-reading, studying, and reciting will become our prophesying. Many of us like to hear certain brothers who are good speakers. This shows that it is not easy to change our mentality, because it is still affected by Christianity.

The apostle John's writings are composed of revelations in visions. Only the New Testament writers have received such revelations in visions from God. They wrote down what they saw in the New Testament, and this has been passed on to us. We have to interpret what they saw. In our crystallization-study of John 1, we pointed out that the Word who was God became flesh (vv. 1, 14). In the flesh He became the Lamb (v. 29), and then in resurrection He became the dove (v. 32). Nathanael recognized Him as the Son of God. The Lord then revealed to Nathanael that He was not only the Son of God but also the Son of Man, on whom the angels of God would ascend and descend (vv. 49-51). We have to study these points, recite them, and then we will be able to speak them. By taking this way, we will be equipped to nourish people with the unsearchable riches of Christ.

ABOUT THE AUTHOR

Witness Lee was born in 1905 in northern China and raised in a Christian family. At age 19 he was fully captured for Christ and immediately consecrated himself to preach the gospel for the rest of his life. Early in his service, he met Watchman Nee, a renowned preacher, teacher, and writer. Witness Lee labored together with Watchman Nee under his direction. In 1934 Watchman Nee entrusted Witness Lee with the responsibility for his publication operation, called the Shanghai Gospel Bookroom.

Prior to the Communist takeover in 1949, Witness Lee was sent by Watchman Nee and his other co-workers to Taiwan to ensure that the things delivered to them by the Lord would not be lost. Watchman Nee instructed Witness Lee to continue the former's publishing operation abroad as the Taiwan Gospel Bookroom, which has been publicly recognized as the publisher of Watchman Nee's works outside China. Witness Lee's work in Taiwan manifested the Lord's abundant blessing. From a mere 350 believers, newly fled from the mainland, the churches in Taiwan grew to 20,000 in five years.

In 1962 Witness Lee felt led of the Lord to come to the United States, settling in California. During his 35 years of service in the U.S., he ministered in weekly meetings and weekend conferences, delivering several thousand spoken messages. Much of his speaking has since been published as over 400 titles. Many of these have been translated into over fourteen languages. He gave his last public conference in February 1997 at the age of 91.

He leaves behind a prolific presentation of the truth in the Bible. His major work, *Life-study of the Bible,* comprises over 25,000 pages of commentary on every book of the Bible from the perspective of the believers' enjoyment and experience of God's divine life in Christ through the Holy Spirit. Witness Lee was the chief editor of a new translation of the New Testament into Chinese called the Recovery Version and directed the translation of the same into English. The Recovery Version also appears in a number of other languages. He provided an extensive body of footnotes, outlines, and spiritual cross references. A radio broadcast of his messages can be heard on Christian radio stations in the United States. In 1965 Witness Lee founded Living Stream Ministry, a non-profit corporation, located in Anaheim, California, which officially presents his and Watchman Nee's ministry.

Witness Lee's ministry emphasizes the experience of Christ as life and the practical oneness of the believers as the Body of Christ. Stressing the importance of attending to both these matters, he led the churches under his care to grow in Christian life and function. He was unbending in his conviction that God's goal is not narrow sectarianism but the Body of Christ. In time, believers began to meet simply as the church in their localities in response to this conviction. In recent years a number of new churches have been raised up in Russia and in many eastern European countries.